Ancient Secrets
Of
Personal Power
Tetragrammaton

Professor Hilton Hotema

ISBN: 978-1-63923-437-0

Printed: October 2022

Cover Art By: Amit Paul

Published and Distributed By:
Lushena Books
607 Country Club Drive, Unit E
Bensenville, IL 60106
www.lushenabks.com

ISBN: 978-1-63923-437-0

Table of Contents

Prologue

For what is a man profited, if he shall gain the whole world, and lose his own Health (*Matthew 16:26*).

The Ruler of the mightiest Kingdom on Earth, in bed with broken health, would gladly give his kingdom for the Good Health of his lowest slave.

Good Health is the very Foundation of Success. And we have heard that Good Health is man's birth-right. That is another grievous error. Good Health is the Reward received by him who earns it.

It is in order to inform the reader that this author knows something about the Rules of Health. He was born February 7, 1878, and now in his 83rd year feels as fit as he did at forty. He had one slight illness of influenza when he was a boy of 10, was never vaccinated nor inoculated, and is extremely fortunate that his body was never poisoned with the vile substances called "medicine."

Who could be more competent than he to teach the great subject of Health to those who appreciate the value of Health. And the pressing need of reliable Health knowledge constrained him to begin fifty years to write on that subject, relating such knowledge as he gained by experience in his quest for that Light which leads none astray.

The author is a graduate of all the drugless schools, and walked away with his diplomas in his hand, wiser in what the doctors know, but disappointed in what he wanted to know.

He was fortunate to be a student under Doctor Willard Carver, who in 1906 founded at Oklahoma City the first charted Chiropractic College in the world, and who was the world's greatest Chiropractor. He died in 1943 at the age of 80.

We discovered that doctors are not taught the rules of Health. They are taught certain methods to treat those who have lost their Health. This means that the doctors know as little about How To Live For Health as do their patients who have lost theirs.

The subject-matter of this work has been the consideration of every eminent pen, from the days of Moses to the present. To say anything strictly new would be impossible; but it is possible to shed more light on what has been said and written by others, by stressing certain vital points which have been passed over lightly, almost unnoticed, because of their commonality and simplicity.

Here is the first big mistake. What would be more common and simple than to plant a tiny seed and watch it grow and produce a beautiful flower? Yet, the greatest scientist cannot duplicate the process, nor logically analyze the details of it.

A certain man lived 120 years, and when he was 108 he wrote a book about it. He knew so little as to the reasons of his longevity that he passed lightly over, with little notice, the vital points responsible for his 120 years in the flesh.

This man, Goddard Diamond, was born in Plymouth, Massachusetts, May 1, 1796, and died in San Francisco in 1916. All of the Presidents of this country, from George Washington down to Woodrow Wilson, lived and labored during the days of Diamond.

His book has been long out of print. We read it fifty years ago. The mention of his case in our writings created a demand for the book. Health Research found a copy after a long search, and has now republished it with a Prologue an an Epilogue by this author.

In the Epilogue we stressed the vital points in Diamond's life which were largely responsible for his longevity, explaining how and why they contributed to his long life.

The libraries of the world are filled with great tomes by leading doctors on the subject of health and the "cure of disease." The doctors who wrote them know so little about the basic principle of their subject, that not one of them lived long enough to draw special attention for his state of longevity. Most of them died comparatively young.

We can destroy with five simple words the value of these books on the subject of "disease and its cure." These words are, REMOVE THE CAUSE OF ILLNESS.

The sad experience of five thousand years proves there is no "disease." Consequently, there is no "cure." The world's great doctors have been made the same statement in different words. In 1835 Doctor Samuel Dickson, of Edinburgh, published a work in which he asserted that all diseases "are one and the same" (*Wilder's History of Medicine 1901*, page 357).

That simple, truthful, factual statement swept into oblivion as frivolous and absurd, the whole complicated and inconsistent classification of diseases, with their multifarious names and stupid distinctions, exposing the horrific system of medical murder and plunder which is supported by centuries of fraudulent teaching, by which a profession of supposedly honorable men has created a false and dangerous psychology of "disease," that sends thousands to early graves each year, while yielding fat profits for its exponents.

There are just two conditions of the body, and they are Good Health and Bad Health. The symptoms of Bad Health are what doctors are trained to study, group together, and give them empty names (diagnosis) which mean nothing, and term them "diseases" that may kill the patient unless treated and "cured" according to the teachings of medical art.

We write from experience and knowledge, not from theory and speculation. For fifteen years we treated in our sanitarium patients from all over the country, the majority of them given up by other doctor as hopeless and incurable. We saved them all, losing not one. In the treatment of them we observed the law of Life as follows:

1. Men can live for weeks without eating, but he stops living when he stops breathing. To preserve health, the air must be in motion and free of pollution. Stagnant air in homes, hospitals, bedrooms, stores, shops, etc., is foul like stagnant pools of water. So he put patients in fresh air, kept in circulation with electric fans.

2. Water is next. The greater part of blood and body consist of fluid. To promote health all water entering the body must be pure and free of all pollutants, and "purifiers" used by health boards. So his patients got pure rain water that had not touched the ground.

3. Greatest freedom of function is next. This is secured by fasting, taking no food but air and water, the two foremost foods for man.

Under this natural, health-building regime, the patients recovered as if by magic.

This Law of Life we learned from the bugs and birds. They are never ill, have no hospitals, no doctors, no drugs, no vaccines, no serums, and yet they are ruled by the same Law that governs man. If we follow that Law, we cannot go astray. That is the Law we teach. There is none better.

Chapter 1
Kingdom Within

The Bible says that the Kingdom is within you (*Luke 17:21*).
The Kingdom includes All, and All means, All. Science confirm what the Bible says. It asserts that Man really contains within himself all the universes, systems, planets and globes, and that was the affirmation of the Ancient Masters, who said: —

"I admonish thee that desirest to dive into the inmost parts of Nature, if that which thou seekest thou fondest not within thee, thou wilt never find it without. So, with a loud voice I proclaim: O, Man, Know Thyself and thou wilt know the Universe."

Science says, "The human frame, as a machine, is perfect. It contains within itself no marks by which we can possibly predict its decay. It is apparently intended to go on forever." — Doctor Munro.

"There is no physiological reason known at present why man should ever die." — Doctor Wm. A. Hammond, late Surgeon General, U.S. Army.

"It is more difficult to explain why a man dies than it is to show that he should live forever." — Doctor A. E. Crews, Edinburgh.

Under the Law of Creation, nothing that is less than perfect can come into existence. Modern science finds that to be the case.

The first living creatures of every kind corresponded to this Law of Perfection when they first appeared an earth. But the power of the law does not extend beyond the point of the origin, and after living creatures come into existence, perfection may be lost by a degenerative process that results from many causes or from a combination of causes.

This accounts for the vanishment of the early animals of gigantic size in the primitive days of living creatures. We know of this by the discovery of their remains in various parts of the world, as explained by Professor Hotema in his work Cosmic Creation.

Due to his more perfect powers of vital adjustment, Man, the climax of Creation, lives on and on, to see the less fortunate forms of animal life come and go with the ages.

The Law of Creation demands correspondence between living creatures and their environment. Scientists who have investigated these matters with clear understanding, assert that as soon as an organism becomes standardized and unable to adjust to the changing conditions of the earth, it perishes and vanishes.

Herbert Spencer made an enlightening statement concerning this subject when he wrote:

"Perfect correspondence would be perfect life. Were there no changes in the environment but such as the organism had adopted changes to meet, and were it never to fail in the efficiency with which it met them, that would be eternal existence and eternal knowledge" *(First Principles)*.

Spencer realized that to exist, to grow, to develop, to progress, to continue to live, there must be constant change, continuous adjustment of the organism to its environment, for standardization is stagnation and leads to death.

The Universe and all living things are constantly undergoing a series of changes, of adjustments, of metamorphosis, and those living things which possess a limited capacity of adjustment, slowly degenerate, die out and disappear.

On the other hand, the experience of millions of years has shown, that when the earth became the home of Man, it became a partner of a being that is not only the King of Life and the Climax of Creation, but is as eternal as the very elements of which the suns, stars, and earth are composed. Professor Hotema declares in his remarkable work, *The Glorious Resurrection,* that Human Life is more eternal than the Sun.

There is overwhelming evidence to show that Man not only goes on while other races of animals perish and vanish, but that he will still continue after the earth itself shall have exploded and disintegrated into the huge dust-cloud of which it was originally formed.

Professor Hotema says in his *Cosmic Creation* that for countless ages the Human Ego floated in the Auriferous Substance over the dark waters of the primitive sea, searching for a suitable spot to materialize and step out into visibility upon the new-born earth *(Genesis 1:2)*.

It is logical to assume that Man had done that before in the distant past, and so will he do it again and again in the distant future, when new plants shall have been born from the vast clouds of incandescent particles whirling in endless space.

Man is still on the earth while the animals of the early days have perished; and he will still be on the earth when all the other animals of this era shall have died and disappeared.

Man will live to see a new world of living creatures some into existence, just as he has lived to see many previous worlds of living creatures appear on the earth, then pass out and become extinct.

All this is due to the fact that Man has practically unlimited powers of adaptation, and to his superior intellect and his greater ability to migrate to a new environment as, if, and when the old one is no longer a suitable place for him. No other animal can match man in these precious properties.

Chapter 2
Perfection Is Within

The Kingdom of All was said by the Ancient Masters to be within, and the experience of thousands of years has proven they were right. And so, we should know better than to search without for the fulfillment of our desires.

But the schools and colleges go the other way. Not one teaches us to search within for that property which would promote health and prolong life. That natural, logical course is rejected because it would not make great and rich the institutions of the land which shaped Man's destiny and rule his life. They were not founded for the betterment of humanity as they falsely claim, but for their own profit and gain.

According to the doctrine of the Ancient Masters, Perfection was the primal state of Man. Under the law, nothing less could come into existence.

Perfection is that rare state which puts Man beyond desire, use and need. It is whole and complete in itself — totality.

Perfection desires nothing, and needs nothing beyond the regular replenishment of its constantly changing elements, and the supply is produced by the same Power that produced Man.

A thing, object, or body is imperfect in proportion to its needs that are not automatically supplied by the Creative Power. Departure from Perfection begins the moment anything occurs to burden the living organism with any substance which is not positively essential to its existence.

Aside from changes in environment, herein lies the primary cause of decline and degeneration. A (1) false desire appears, which creates (2) need, which creates (3) use, which creates (4)

4

habit, which creates (5) vital adjustment, which creates (6) demand, which creates (7) enslavement, which creates (8) degeneration, which (9) creates death.

And the schools and colleges, for profit and gain, falsely teach that this course is progress, and stupid man believes it. He is going to progress beyond Perfection, and thinks that is improvement. That is what he is taught by the sordid institutions that live on darkness and thrive on ignorance. He has heard of the Kingdom Within, but thinks that is just poetry for childish minds.

What did Man need, when he was created, that was not Within the Kingdom? Nothing but Air.

"Every living thing must breathe the air in order to live. The tree breathes the air through its leaves. The leaves are in this sense the lungs of the tree. Insects breathe the air through the openings in their bodies. Frogs breathe the air partly through their skin. Fishes breathe the air by taking oxygen from the water as it passes over their gills. Man breathes the air through the air cells of his lungs." Frederick M. Rossiter, B.S., M.D., L.C.R.P., London.

"Living is actually a struggle for air. Keep the vast lung surface of the body supplied with fresh air, and observe all other health rules, and there is, scientifically speaking, no known reason why man should ever die." (Professor J. S. Haldane of England, in *Respiration*).

"Hardly any one understands this science (of breathing), which all should know and practice. It is the air that renews our blood and carries vitality to all our organs. It is the air that helps to give us balance and to keep our physical and psychic functions in proper order. Most men use only a third, a quarter, or even a fifth part of the lungs' total surface" (Professor Edmond Szekely).

Various theories have been advanced by science to explain the cause of aging and dying. One of the latest is that of Doctor Ross A. McFarland, Professor of environmental Health and Safety at the Harvard School of Public Health. He opines that aging results from a decreasing supply of Oxygen in the body. He found that subjects, when deprived of Oxygen, lost capacity for sensation, perception and judgment. "These symptoms," said he, "parallel those in aging persons."

The respiratory capacity increases from about the 15th to the 35th year, and then it diminishes at the rate of about one and a half cubic inches per year. This means the capacity of respiration of a man of 60 would be about 30 cubic inches less than that of a man of 40, of the same height and weight (Hutchinson.)

Why the decrease? Lung cells ruined by polluted air, and respiratory capacity lost by lack of exercise to make one breathe deeply. Szekely stated that "most men use only a third, a quarter, or even a fifth part of the lungs' total surface."

Breathing from birth is not only an essential function, but a life-long process. Living is breathing, and the death of the body comes with the last feeble exhalation.

Eating and drinking are voluntary, controlled functions. Respiration is an automatic, involuntary process, so far beyond man's conscious control that he breathes when unconscious in sleep, or from injury, even better and deeper, more regularly and rhythmically, than when conscious and awake.

Respiration is the primal function of the organism. All other functions are secondary, and designed to keep the body fit to perform respiration.

The lungs are definitely designed for and adapted to their work. The stomach is simply an enlargement of the alimentary canal and nothing more. The lungs are specific organs, largest by far in the body, filling the thorax from collar bone to lower-most ribs, and from sternum in front to spine in back. They are strictly the Organs of Life. When we stop breathing we stop living; and when man dies, he goes gasping for air. Man cannot die as long as he can breathe.

In the beginning of Man on the earth plane, air was his only need that was external to the Kingdom Within, and all his other needs rose from unnatural desires that created vital adjustment. And the air man needed was free and abundant, requiring for its possession no other labor than that of breathing.

This means that Breatharianism is Physical Perfection. The Bible shows that Man came into earthly existence a Breatharian. The Breath of Life supplied all the requirements of his organism. Nothing else was lacking, and nothing else was needed. The air he breathed, and nothing more, sustained his organism and he lived for centuries. That was the Golden Age of Man.

Modern science has discovered that there is sufficient ELECTRICITY in one breath of air to power a large air-plane for a month. Why do we mention Electricity?

That question gets a surprising answer from Professor Hotema in his work titled *The Flame Divine*. That answer will startle the reader.

The less Man needs the more he becomes like gods, who use nothing and are immortal — said the Ancient Masters.

Want, poverty, sickness, degeneration, all rise from the faulty work of Man. He reaps as he sows. These are the natural products of his sowing, his habits which correspond with his desires. He increases his burdens as he increases his wants. And the sordid institutions which live and thrive on human wants, are constantly working to increase those wants.

Advanced scholars point out that there would have been in Man's physical beginning no unfilled wants; otherwise physical existence had been impossible. They show by Logical reasoning that the only way to improve physical man, is to reduce his wants and decrease his economic burden.

But the schools are not interested in any course that (1) raises Man to a higher plane and (2) eliminates his wants. For nothing must be allowed to be done that will disturb the nicely planned and fixed order of civilization.

Every brand and department of government that rules the people, leads away from Perfection. The movement away begins with the child in school and continues throughout life without a stop. School life is largely a process of mind conditioning.

This statement was well attested on January 12, 1951, when Frank W. Abrams, Chairman of the Board, Standard Oil Co. of New Jersey, made an address before the National Citizens Commission for Public Schools, which was published and widely circulated at the time.

Among other things, he said:

"There can be no doubt that we are talking about something very fundamental to business when we talk about education. . . If only to maintain and expand its markets, the business world has at least as big a stake as anyone in the achievement of an educated, productive and tolerant society. There is a definite correlation between education and the consumption of commodities. Education has done more to create markets for business than any other force in America.

There it is direct from the business world. We see that one big purpose of education is to maintain and expand the markets of business, and to create a demand for commodities, while not a word is said about promoting Health and prolonging Life. And while billions of dollars are expended annually in the education of the children of America, the purpose is not for the betterment of humanity but for the promotion of business.

The act and science of natural, healthful living are so lightly regarded, that they receive little attention. He who is so far ahead of the multitude as to oppose the social pattern by teaching the Law of Creation, is promptly silenced, disgraced and liquidated. And the press carries large headlines, proclaiming that another enemy of social progress has been found and jailed for the protection of the People. And the mind-conditioned masses believe it.

One's teaching may be in perfect accord with the Law of Creation, but such teaching fails to harmonize with civilization's artificial world, or to support its social pattern, hence it cannot be accepted or tolerated by any institution or any form of government. It must be and it is crushed "for the good of the people."

Tell us how long Man's treated wants and unnatural desires will mean profit for Commercialism, and we'll tell you how long Man will remain in his present state of degeneracy and economic slavery.

It will surprise the orthodox and the mind-conditioned masses to be told that as man moves back from his vaunted "progress" toward Primal Perfection, his health improves, his life lengthens, his wants decline, and his economic burden decreases.

9

We thus learn what these burdens, are, when they came, and what they do to humanity. We see them as the product of Man's created wants and unnatural desires which Perfect Man had not, and that's why he was perfect. Man has produced them, and he can destroy them. They have produced his miserly, and he wants to keep them and find remedies and cures for the misery they produce.

Not until Man began to form habits and adopt practices which created wants and unnatural desires, did he begin to decline and degenerate. He was deceived then, as he is now, by the illusion of process as he developed new habits and increased his wants. He believed then, as he does now, that each new invention was a sign of progress, while he and his doctors were sorely puzzled by the fact that his health continued to decline and his life-span to decrease. We can remedy all this, shouts Medical Art, if more money is supplied for "medical research."

Economic freedom is the first step back toward Men's high estate of Primal perfection. Every animal, in its native state, has economic freedom. Man is the only economic slave and sickly creature on the earth. He has made himself what he is by his unnatural wants and acquired desires, and only he can correct the distressing situation.

In complete freedom from every want, to be dependent upon nothing but what the Law of Creation supplies, then Man's mind and senses are under control. He is released from the consequences of action, which are the bonds and chains that bind down those who are the slaves of want and desire.

It is well at this point to introduce to the student the great work on Breatherianism with some vital statements excerpted therefrom on...

Perfection Within

Living is breathing. When you stop breathing you stop living, no matter how good your heart may be. Most cases of death from so-called heart failure are due to the paralyzation of the breathing center in the brain by polluted air.

The network of blood capillaries in the lungs are distributed everywhere in the tiny spaces between the billions of air vesicles, and envelope their walls within a vascular screen.

The blood flows through the lungs in billions of small streams, almost in direct contact with the air in the lungs. It is as though the River of Living Water were sprayed through the Breath of Life in a very fine shower of Red Mist, so that every drop of Blood and every particle of air in the lungs are brought together in the closest possible proximity.

1. The blood, from all parts of the body, goes to the heart and then directly to the lungs. This blood is a dark blue in color, approaching to black, and is saturated through and through with all the waste, filth, and pollution collected from all the cells, tissues, organs, glands and blood vessels.

2. This blood is a deadly stream of poison in the broadest sense of the word. Unless the process of purification occurs quickly, without undue delay, death soon ensues, and the doctor would say, "heart attack."

3. As the purifying process occurs in the lungs, a surprising change takes place in the color of the blood. At the moment when the poisoned blood passes into the air-cells of the lungs, a lightning exchange occurs between the blood and the air, in

which the color of the blood becomes scarlet, due to the passage of the poison in the blood into the air-cells of the lungs, and eliminated from the body as invisible vapor in the process of exhalation.

4. This is the only process of Blood Purification in the world, and results from the blood exchanging its poisonous gases for the air gases in the lungs. This occurs approximately 2,880 times every 24 hours, in which time approximately 125 barrels of blood are purified in the lungs.

This data tells us why it is so highly important to know that the air we breathe is not polluted. But where do we find air that is not polluted? If you live in the city you live in and breathe polluted air. When you drive on the highways, you are in a mass of polluted air. The fumes of your cookery in your home, and the smokers in your family, fill your home with polluted air.

A great physician in Paris declared in the 19th century that of all the causes of human ailments, vitiated air is the leader.

In the polluted air of this civilization, where a breath of really pure air cannot be found, when the poisoned blood stream in your body flows to the lungs for purification, no purification can take place. There is simply an exchange of poisonous gases.

Professor Hotema covered this subject in particular in his work in 1923, titled *Unity & Simplicity of Disease*, now sold out and out of print. That is another reason why he devoted special attention to the subject in his great work titled *Man's Higher Consciousness,* Which, should be studied by every person.

Other related works the student should study are *The Facts of Nutrition and Fasting Story* #II by Professor Hotema. He will be amazed to learn that even now, there are people in the world who live without eating.

Chapter 3
Secrets of the Body

It is in order to notice a state so vital in Man's life, that it is responsible for his continuity upon the earth while other living creatures perish and vanish. And yet this important, mysterious condition is so lightly regarded by medical art that my systematic research has ever been made to determine how it operates or what effects it has upon the organs and glands of the body.

One of the greatest anthropologists of this century, Doctor Alexis Carrel, in his remarkable book, *Man The Unknown*, gave to the world the best data on this subject that have ever come to our attention, and we can do no better than to notice some of the things he said.

Carrel pointed to the important fact that the cause of evolution is the inherent quality of all living organisms toward a higher level of development. This natural, persistent urge, in order to preserve the body and prolong its existence, results in the adjustment of the organism to its environment and to the evil habits of man.

Said Carrel: "There is a striking contrast between the durability of a body and the transitory character of its elements. Man is composed of a soft, alterable material, susceptible of disintegrating in a few hours; but he lasts longer (on that account) than if made of steel. Not only does he last, but he constantly overcomes the difficulties and dangers of the outside world (environment). He accommodates himself, much better than (all) other animals do, to the changing conditions of his environment. He persists in living, despite physical, economic and social upheavals.

"Such endurance is due to a particular mode (and change) of activity in his tissues and humors. The body seems to mold itself on events. Instead of wearing out (disintegrating) it changes. Our organs always improvise means of meeting every new situation; and these means are such that they tend to give us a maximum (prolonged) duration (life).

"The physiological processes, which are the substratum of inner time (aging process), always incline in the direction leading to the longest survival of the individual. This strange function, this watchful automatism, with its specific characters, makes possible human existence. It is called adaptation" (pages 191-2).

This extraordinary, automatic ability of the organism is responsible for Man's being on the earth today, after having lived to see pass into oblivion of the animals, including the giant Dinosaur, which were on the earth when he first emerged as a visible being from the Invisible Realm, as Professor Hotema related in his *Cosmic Creation*.

This amazing condition of Vital Adjustment is erroneously and stupidly called Vital Resistance by medical art, the purpose of which falsity is to deceive both doctors and laymen with its tricky terminology, invented to provide a place for the doctor, his vaccines and serums.

The Law of Vital Adjustment may properly be extended to include the Law of Cure, as Carrel stated in his book. For it is this inherent power which sustains the body in health when its course is UNOBSTRUCTED, and which RESTORES the sick body to health, if restoration occurs at all. And, as a rule, this restoration must take place by overcoming the blundering, hindering, damaging work of the doctor and his dangerous methods and poisonous remedies.

Scientifically speaking, the proper term of the Law of Adjustment is the Law of Correspondence, concerning which the great evolutionist, Herbert Spencer, wrote:

"Perfect Correspondence would be Perfect Life. Were there no changes in the environment but such as the organism had adapted changes to meet, and were it never to fail in the efficiency with which it meet them, there would be eternal existence and eternal knowledge" (First Principles).

Of Spencer's observations, Henry Drummond said:

"He is analyzing with minute care the relations between Environment and Life (Not Life but the body). He unfolds the principles according to which Life is high or low, long or short, showing why organisms live and why they die. And finally he defines a (perfect) condition of things in which an organism (not Life) would never die — in which it would enjoy a perpetual and perfect life" (in the flesh) (*Natural Law in the Spiritual World*).

In his work, *Celestial Correspondence* (1926), Coulson Turnbull refers to this condition, calling it the Science of Correspondence, and, in tracing back to fundamentals, he finds that this is actually the Science of Astrology, the only Science of Man the world has ever had, which "reveals the meaning and time arrangement of electrons, atoms, molecules, cells, their creation, motion and related position to one another, whether in nebulae, star, sun, archangel, or atom. The Law of the Universe is one, constantly repeated by the ancient Seers, Masters and Adepts" (page 12).

Returning to Carrel, he said: "All physiological activities are endowed with the property of being adaptive. Adaptation, therefore, assumes innumerable aspects. But these aspects may be grouped into two categories, intra-organic and extra-organic.

"Intra-organic adaptation is responsible for the constancy of the organic medium and of the relations of tissues and humors. It brings about the automatic repair of tissues and the cure of disease."

There we have it, direct from one of the greatest medical doctors of modern times, THE LAW OF CURE, leaving no place for the doctor, his treatment and remedies. He continued:

"Extra-organic adaptation adjusts the individual to the physical, psychological, and economic world. It enables him to survive in spite of the unfavorable conditions of his environment (and his evil habits, and the poisonous remedies of medical art).

"Upon these two aspects (disregarded by medical art), the adaptive functions are at work during each instant of our whole life. They are the indispensable basis of our duration" (page 192).

Now we can begin to see why this great scientist was "kicked out" of the Rockefeller Institute of Medical Research very soon after the publication of his book, in which he bluntly said:

"The more eminent the (medical) specialist, the more dangerous he is — Medicine has been paralyzed by the narrowness of its doctrines" (pages 46, 283).

Evil environment and evil habits have caused man's body to suffer great and serious adjustment, in order to survive, from its primal perfection, causing a loss of many of its higher powers, which fade out first.

Traces and marks of the changes that have occurred in the body's structures and functions, due to such adjustment, appear to a blind science in the form of more — than a hundred organs and glands, now dormant or semi dormant, which were originally functional and useful, but now practically useless and functionless, which means a loss of physiological activities and psychical powers that has reduced man to a very low level of Consciousness.

And a stupid science regards these dormant organs and vestigial glands as signs which indicate man's ascension from the ape stage. Contemplate if you can the destiny of him who is led by that kind of science. Or by a religious system which declares that God so loved the world, just a tiny speck in space, that he gave his only begotten, Son, just another human being, that whosoever believeth in him should not perish, but have everlasting life (*John 3:16*). No law involved; Life is ruled by what a man believes.

We pick up a publication and in it see an advertisement, with pictures of great men of past ages, who were noted for their remarkable ability, and with this question: "What Secret Power did they possess?"

These men rose above the multitude because of the possession and the good use of those qualities which most individuals have lost as a result of physical and mental degeneration, and a system of medical treatment for illness which has been condemned as dangerous by the best doctors of the land.

Consciousness

We are what our Consciousness is, and Professor Hotema, in his work titled *Man's Higher Consciousness*, gives the reader an inkling of what *Man's Higher Consciousness,* gives the reader an inkling of what Man was competent to do ages before the state of Vital Adjustment, made necessary by his evil habits and the artificial, destructive condition called "civilization," reduced him to the lowly level of Consciousness which now generally prevails.

Man's state of Consciousness can be no better than the state of his body.

"Man's body, serving as radio and television on the physical plane, is composed of trillions of cells, each cell being composed of millions of atoms, and each atom a miniature solar system, with "planets" in the form of electrons and protons, revolving at tremendous speed round a common center of attraction, the nucleus.

Each atom and each cell in the body is Intelligized by Cosmic Consciousness and Vitalized by Cosmic Force. Through the Infinite Atom man's Consciousness comes directly from the Cosmic Source, and is limited by his limited capacity to receive and express it.

This is the Secret Power, almost unknown, which rules men and arranges them in many classes, from the highest to the lowest. Those of each class manifest a state of Intelligence according to the condition of their body, the radio. The better the body's condition, the greater the Intelligence it will manifest. There is no known way to put much Intelligence into the degenerate brain of a dunce.

There in a nutshell is the secret why certain men possess greater powers of Consciousness than others do. It is not a question of attuning ourselves to the "Wisdom of the Ages," as stated by the advertisements in the magazines, but of improving the state of the body, the instrument of reception and manifestation.

We should be wise and treat our body as we do our radio and television set when they fail to function. We have them repaired by a competent mechanic who knows his business. But where would we find a doctor who is competent to repair a body which he knows so little that he cannot make even one drop of blood, nor explain how the body makes it.

Every doctor who treats the sick should be a Creationist, a Naturist, an Astrologist, an Anthropologist, a Biologist, a Psychologist, and a Physiologist. Then he would know what he is doing in treating the sick and why he is doing it. For he would then know that illness is not a foe to be combatted, but a friend to be carefully aided.

It would appear a little short of ludicrousness to suggest to the brainwashed, mind-conditioned masses that birds and beasts possess a higher degree of Consciousness than does modern man; but such are the findings of unprejudiced experts in the field of psycho-bio-physiology.

Some facts on these things, discovered and recorded by unbiased researchers, are presented by Professor Hotema in his work titled *Man's Higher Consciousness*, in which he describes a high degree of Consciousness in the lower animals that is in-explicable and enigmatical to physical science.

These experts have attempted to analyze the peculiar Consciousness of migratory fowls that fly great distances in the fall, sometimes non-stop, over hundreds of miles of Open Ocean, returning in the spring by entirely different routes to the very spots from which they departed months before.

Deslandres said that the homing-sense of birds appears to be the quality of an electric perception. Nothing strange about that, for all perception by living organisms is electrical, as we shall show in Chapter 8. This is what Deslandres said,

"Birds can home over territory that offers no visible landmarks. I've seen a pigeon released from a balloon 5000 feet high. The bird was carried in a closed box. As soon as released, it rapidly described two circles around the balloon and then, without hesitation, darted off in the direction of its dove-cot, 250 miles away.

Mr. A. W. Neal, his wife and three children, lived in Owensboro, Ky. They had a dog, called Lassie, and had owned him since he was a pup. In September, 1959, the family removed to Los Angeles, leaving Lassie with Mr. Neal's brother, in Owensboro, to be shipped to them later when they were settled.

The children cried when Lassie was left behind, and Lassie was sad too. The family had been gone from Owensboro about a month when the dog disappeared. He was also going to Los Angeles.

As Mr. Neal was in downtown Los Angeles in March, 1960, he chanced to see a brown dog running toward him. It was Lassie. He called the dog, and it ran up and jumped at him. Neal was astounded. He said, "I couldn't believe it."

Lassie had found his friends 2000 miles away, in a place where he had never been before. He had travelled for weeks over mountains and desert, across rivers and through cities, in the winter times.

That event to us, with our limited, five-sense-powers, seems like a miracle. But it is common to birds and beasts with their seven-sense-powers.

In Chapter 8 we shall show that the science of psycho-bio-physiology rests upon the evidence of the astral realm, the world invisible to us on the limited five-sense-plane. In the case of living creatures with the sixth and seventh sense powers in action, the element called distance (space) obstructs nothing. They can detect vibratory waves unknown on the five-sense-plane.

The Bible mentions the Seven Powers in allegorical terms. It refers to a Lamb with Seven Horns and Seven Eyes, which are the Seven Spirits sent forth into all the world (*Revelation 5:6*), but only Five of them appear in action in most men. The horns and the eyes represent the Seven Astral Powers of Action and the Seven Astral Powers of Perception, says Professor Hotema in *Son of Perfection*.

Our conscious knowledge results from electrical waves of vibration. The whole scheme of materialism, whether animals or rocks, suns or planets, is reducible in the ultimate to one single existence waves of Astral Light or Cosmic Electricity. What we think we hear, see, feel, smell, taste, exists only as vibratory waves, as we shall show in Chapter 8.

The body is our tomb and our eyes are the windows of our tomb. Our ears are the radio of our tomb; our function of feeling brings emotions to our tomb; and odors and flavors enter our tomb over our nerves and the effect is registered in the brain.

And our physical apparatuses deceive us by making things appear the opposite of what they really are. This accounts for most of the errors that create the confusion in which physical scientists live and labor, traveling in a circle but never getting any nearer to the center, and calling that "progress."

We regard the visible world as being external to us. But all we know of that world is registered within us, within our brain, within the Kingdom (*Luke 17:21*).

Damage the brain and we may still live, but we'd have no conscious knowledge of anything but our own existence, and may be not that much.

Damage the brain less, and our conscious knowledge expands accordingly. And give us the undamaged brain of the bird, and our conscious knowledge of the world would be the equal of that of the birds.

And thus we observe that we do not rise in Consciousness by attuning ourselves to the Wisdom of the Ages, but by the improvement of the Tomb in which we, the God of the earth, dwell upon the earth plane.

Yes, the God of the whole earth, with dominion over every living thing, and with a degenerate brain that reduces him to the lowest level of Consciousness of all the animals upon the earth.

Man is conscientized by vibratory impressions, received as Astral Light or Cosmic Electricity, direct from the Universal Source, and this makes modern man, in his present degenerate state, very low in the scale of Consciousness. Listen again to what the great Carrel said:

"Our civilizations, like those preceding it, has created certain conditions of existence ... render life itself impossible ... Since the natural conditions of existence have been destroyed by modern civilization, the science of man has become the most necessary of all sciences.

"Before beginning this work (book), the author realized its difficulty, its almost impossibility. He undertook it merely because somebody had to. For men cannot (continue to) follow modern civilization along its present course, as they are (constantly) degenerating. They have been fascinated by the revelations of the sciences of inert matter. They have not understood that their body and consciousness are subjected to natural laws, more obscure than, but as inexorable as, the laws of the sidereal world.

"We are beginning to realize the weakness of our civilization. Many want to shake off the dogmas imposed upon them by modern society. This book has been written for them, and also for those who are old enough to understand the necessity not only of mental, political, (religious), and social changes, but of the overthrow of industrial (and religious) civilization and of the advent of another conception of human progress" (Preface, pages xiii-xv, page 28).

Strong and pointed language, coming from one standing so high in the world, and knowing so well what we have and what he was saying. And that "civilization" against which he uttered this bitter blast, did not take those well-directed blows "on the chin" in a calm, peaceful attitude. For within nine years after his book appeared, Carrel died suddenly in prison of a "heart attack."

Man today is dependent upon his five physical senses to contact the Astral Light of the Cosmos, and these senses are more or less degenerate and deficient, while his Five Astral Senses of the Kingdom of the God Within have been dormantized and rendered practically useless by the polluted air of his environment, as Professor Hotema shows in *"Man's Higher Consciousness,"* in which work the student will learn about the Holy Seat of the God Within the Five Chambers of the Golden Bowl.

(*Ecclesiastes 12:6*), and the function of these Holy Chambers is still unknown to modern science.

These Five Chambers the Ancient Masters called the Five Stars of the Microcosm, and they are symbolized in various ways in the ancient scriptures by certain Fives, as the Five Golden Emeralds, the Five Loaves, etc. — *Matthew 14:17*).

The Sankhys doctrine stated that the Five Physical Senses of conscious man are the exteriorized products of the five corresponding Astral Chambers in the Golden Bowl, and these are listed and described by Professor Hotema in *"Man's Higher Consciousness."*

Who can 'he found in the polluted air of this civilization with undamaged, functional Astral Chambers in his Golden Bowl?

The first organ that reacts to polluted air is the nose, and the reaction is called a "simple cold." Yes, simple, but a sign of great importance. It appears in infancy and continues as long as one lives in the polluted air of civilization.

The polluted air ruins the Astral Chambers, sending down to a very low level the Consciousness of Man, as shown by Hotema in *Man's Higher Consciousness.*

Chapter 4
The Mysterious Glands

The skillfully prepared propaganda of the big book sellers proclaims in persuasive tones that we must attune ourselves to the Wisdom of the Ages if we would acquire the Secret Power that leads to the Path of Success.

The class caught by that brand of bait constitutes the mind — conditioned masses that fail to learn the trick of thinking. For the thinker realizes that the proper move to make is to discover how and where those Masters got their Knowledge who gave the world the Wisdom of the Ages. And where else would we search for that Secret but in the Brain, the marvelous Organ that lifted up to a High Level of consciousness those Masters who gave the world this Ageless Wisdom.

Of that mysterious Dynamo of the Human Organism the eminent Anthropologist and Biologist, Doctor Alexis Carrel, said — "Our intelligence can no more realize the immensity of the Brain than the extent of the sidereal Universe" (*Man the Unknown*, page 95).

Science informs us that the most intelligent men of the race utilize only ten percent of their cranial capacity, which means that the best of us are 90% ignorant.

The Ancient Masters taught that we are what our Consciousness is, and our State of Consciousness is governed by the activity of the Brain. This means that the Consciousness exercised by the best of us is 90% below the maximum level.

This fact makes it easier for us to understand the amazing Consciousness of the fowls of the air, as mentioned in the preceding chapter, and should direct us where to search for the ways and means of increasing our Consciousness and expanding our knowledge of ourselves and of the world in which we live.

The Bible also aids us in this quest by stating that the Kingdom of God is within (*Luke 17:21*). Then, where else but within should we search for the great things we want? And why do our leaders and teachers ignore this ancient advice? Simply because to do otherwise would upset their clever schemes of controlling the masses.

Within The Organism

Aristotle, the famous Greek sage and philosopher, related in his *"Book of Secrets"* that — "There is a medicine called the ineffable glory and treasure of philosophers, which completely rectifies the whole body."

Where shall we find that Elixir of Life? Man, science and medical art make the mistake of looking for it in some brew or concoction that comes from without. Perhaps some strange herb growing wild in the Himalayas. Or the mineral salts and vitamins of commercialism. Or the "wonder drugs" of medical art. But Aristotle knew better. He said that — "It lay within the body, waiting only for human intelligence to make it available."

We realize that few will follow us now, when we direct the Mind to the centers within the Kingdom of God where the Elixir of Life is generated, being guided in this course by the fact that thousands of years before the days of Aristotle, the Ancient Masters said:

"Man shall renew his Youth like the eagles (by the use of the substances generated within the Kingdom of God. For we shall "ask now the beasts, and they shall teach thee; and the fowls of the air, and they shall tell thee" (*Psalms 103:5; Job 12:7, 12*).

Aristotle knew that the great things which men most desire come from within, not from without. He found that secret in the teachings of the great Hermes of Egypt; and modern science has at long last discovered a little of what the Ancient Masters knew so well.

Behold, within the realm of the marvelous Endocrine Glands of the body lies the glory and treasure of Creation which completely rectifies the organism, promotes its vitality, increases its consciousness, and prolongs its days.

Yes, at long last one valuable discovery has actually been made by our boasted science. It has found that the Endocrine Glands are the Master Chemists of the organism. What their products do has amazed the world of science. For these products stimulate the functional activity of all the vital organs, which function properly only in response to such stimulation, while the Endocrines themselves receive their own stimulation direct from the Cranial and Abdominal Brains.

By the aid of our late discoveries we have finally been able to interpret some of the strange symbols and puzzling parables of the Ancient Scriptures, and have thus discovered that the Ancient Masters possessed profound knowledge on the subject of Endocrinology. Yet, it is only within the last half century that our boasted science has found the very first nuggets of this precious knowledge in the rich lodes of Creation's Golden Hills, uncovering secrets of the body which not only enable us to begin dimly to interpret these ancient symbols and parables, but amaze us to behold how far ahead of us the masters were in the Science of Anthropology, Biology, Psychology and Physiology, a field in which we have practically no science at all, according to the declarations of our greatest scientists in this field of research.

A small group of occult students, by the aid of this newer knowledge, has been astonished to find that the last book of the Bible is devoted exclusively to the physiological processes of the body on a plane of Consciousness so far above anything we have ever known, that it fills us with embarrassment and humiliation to see our sad error in believing that the Book of Revelation treated, as the noted mystic Swedenborg wrote, "not at all of worldly things, but of heavenly things; not of empires and kingdoms, but of heaven and the church.

No wonder the clergy, after sixteen hundred years of study and effort, have never been able to make any sense out of Revelation. The Preface of Swedenborg's book of 1200 pages on Revelation, ends with this statement:

"Everyone can see that the Apocalypse can by no means be explained but by the Lord alone; for each word therein contains arcana, which would in no wise be known without a particular enlightenment, and thus revelation; on which account it has pleased the 'Lord to open the sight of my (Swedenborg's) spirit, and to teach me.

"Do not believe, therefore, that I have taken anything herein from myself, nor from any angel, but from the Lord alone. The Lord also said to John through, the angel, 'Seal not the words of the prophecy of this Book' (Chapter 22:10); by which it means that they are to be made manifest."

Old Swedenborg was not shy nor modest in the matter of casting bouquets at himself and professing to be on such intimate terms with the Lord. And his "Lord" knew as little about the subject-matter of Revelation as the clergy, as shown by Professor Hotema in his work titled *Son of Perfection*.

Hotema shows that the Apocalypse deals, in symbol and parable, with the fable of the Garden of Eden mentioned in the first chapters of Genesis, and follows up by Showing that this fable treats of the deepest functions of the Endocrine Glands of the body.

Now, think of the fraudulent manner in which the Pious Church Fathers have knowingly and deliberately presented to the world at large as theological dogma, the Sacred Scriptures of the Masters that refer to no God but Man, and deal with certain psycho-bio-physiologic, processes of the body.

And then see what else these crocks did: They took the head-sign of the Ancient Zodiac, Aries the Ram, and changed it to the Lamb of God, thus inventing the "only begotten Son, that whosoever believeth in him should not perish, but have everlasting life" (*John 1:29; 3:16*).

A few occult students now know that the Apocalypse is the Great Parable of the Bible. Of it, one noted author said: "The Apocalypse is one of the most stupendous allegories ever penned by the hand of man."

Discovery of Endocrinology

Doctor Theophile Bordeu of Paris appears as the first in modern time in the field of Endocrinology. In 1776 he published two small volumes, titled *"Researches into the Mucous Tissues or Cellular Organs,"* and the other, *"Analysis of The Blood."*

He began with observations on the characteristics of eunuchs and capons, also on spayed female animals. He recorded the conception of sexual secretions, taken up by the blood, that give to male or female the maleness or femaleness of character of the individual. How accurate was his observation and how shrewd his reasoning which led to his conclusions, are clearly evident from the findings of modern research on this subject.

And then the marvelous discoveries of this doctor received no notice from medical art because no pecuniary possibilities were presented. And so the secret of the Endocrines languished in darkness until a literary as well as a physiological genius in Paris, Claude Bernard, began to dilate on which he termed the internal and external secretions of the glands of the body, emphasizing the marked difference between them.

Then in 1855-6 came the publication of Bernard's *"Lectures on Experimental Physiology,"* and the effect of this was such as to move medical art, and a systematic study of the Endocrines and their function followed.

The Abdominal Brain is termed the Progenital or Reproductive Center. But this term is incomplete in that it suggests only one function. While it is true that Reproduction is its best known function, there is another not so well known to science, but equally as important, if not even more so from the viewpoint of the individual.

It was chiefly to this latter and little-known angle that the Ancient Masters, those "superstitious heathens of antiquity," devoted so much work and attention, because of its high importance to the individual, that they came to be called Sex Worshippers by those who desired to discredit them, and phallic symbols in ancient art came to be quite common on that account.

This secondary and mysterious function of the Pelvic Dynamo of the Organism is what the Masters discovered to be of primal importance in the development of Man's Higher Consciousness.

After years of research, the Masters found that the elements of these internal secretions, when absorbed by the blood and not consumed in masturbation or fornication, impart to man his masculinity, his virility, his quality of leadership, and even his nature as God of the earth in all respects, not inferior to the fowls or the beasts in his Powers of Consciousness.

And here was Aristotle's "ineffable glory and treasure of philosophers, which completely rectifies the whole body."

The particular group of glands with which we are not mostly concerned, are those termed ductless. While not served with ducts to convey their products to a definite part of the body, they pour their products directly into the blood stream, by which the products are conveyed to all parts of the body. In this way an unhealthy condition of one or more of these glands, or the unlawful consumption of their products, affects the whole body.

The glands most intimately involved include (1) the pineal and (2) pituitary in the brain, (3) the thyroid and parathyroid in the neck, (4) the thymus in the thorax, (5) the suprarenal's in the abdomen, (6) the prostate and epididymis in the pelvis, and (7) the gonads in the scrotum. This leads directly to that mysterious Book with Seven Seals mentioned in the Bible (Revelation 5).

The book of Revelation was compiled from a Hindu scroll that was written thousands of years before the world ever heard of the gospel Jesus, which means that all mention of him in Revelation are fraudulent interpolations of the biblical makers.

This Hindu scroll was given to the great Pythagorean philosopher of the first century, Apollonius of Tyana, when he visited India about 45 A.D. On his return to Asia Minor he retired to the isle of Patmos and made a copy of the scroll, interpolating certain statements to make the work harmonize with the conditions of his country and the customs of his people.

He went to India for the purpose of studying the Hindu religions system, and spent the rest of the days of his 98 years in teaching that system to his people.

He was such a remarkable man that the people worshipped him as a god after his death. The Roman Emperors, in his lifetime, sought him for advice, and after his death, they adorned their temples with statues of this greatest philosopher and teacher of the Roman Empire.

Then came the establishment of the Roman Catholic Church in the 4th century, and the Church Fathers compiled their New Testament from the voluminous writings of Apollonius, going so far as to make him the Jesus of the Gospels, the Paul of the Epistles, and the John of Revelation, according to the writings of J. M. Roberts, a wise American lawyer, whose manuscript was published in 1894, after his death, and titled *Antiquity Unveiled*, now a very rare book.

Chapter 5
The Seven Astral Centers

In the Hindu scroll which became the Last book of the Bible, the Seven Vital Centers of the organism were given special names, as follows:

1. Muladhara (sacral plexus)
2. Svadhishthana (prostatic plexus)
3. Manipura (solar plexus)
4. Anahata (cardiac plexus)
5. Vishuddha (pharyngeal plexus)
6. Ajna (cavernous plexus)
7. Sahasrara (conarium plexus)

Here are the Seven Secret Reasons why the last Book of the Bible has been called the Book of Sevens. These Sevens are mentioned again and again in various ways, all of which Professor Hotema has explained in his *Son of Perfection*.

As the symbols and parables of Revelation deal definitely with these Seven Major Nerve Ganglia of the organism, and not with heaven and the church, he who would learn how to increase his Consciousness, and control, influence and dominate others, should familiarize himself with them and learn how to develop them to a high degree. For here we have one of the top secrets of the Sacred Wisdom of the Ancient Masters on which are based the teachings of the Scriptures.

We shall disclose to the reader how stupid and misleading it is to literalize the statements in the Bible, and show him how the Masters, who prepared the Ancient Scrolls, wove into their work symbols and allegories that were baffling to the exoteric but clearly understood by the esoteric.

The Seven Great Ganglionic Centers of man's body mentioned above, were described in Revelation as Seven Synagogues in Asia (Minor), the native land of him who was the copyist. They are called Churches in the Bible, but the copyist never heard of a Church. To him the Temples were known as Synagogues. This is more evidence to show the great liberties the Biblical makers exercised in compiling their Book they blamed on God (Revelation 1:4).

The ancient scribe, who was Apollonius in this case, named the Seven Synagogues: (1) Ephesus (2) Smyrna, (3) Pergamos, (4) Thyatira, (5) Sardis, (6) Philadelphia, and (7) Laodicea (Rev. 1:11).

The cities of the Seven Synagogues were on the mainland, not far from the isle of Patmos, where sat the author as he copied the Hindu Scrolls.

These cities were selected because of some well-known characteristic, or something for which each city was noted, thus calling to mind of the esoteric the somatic center it represented. The cities are listed in the same order in the Apocalypse as are the Chakras in the Hindu Upanishads.

1. Muladhara, the sacral ganglion, is represented by Ephesus. This center is at the base of the spinal cord, being thus at the power pole of the cerebro-spinal system, and the upward starting-point of the Living Fire.

This city was celebrated for its great temple of Diana (Cybele), the "many breasted mother," who appears in the Apocalypse as the "Women clothed with the Sun, the moon underneath her feet" (*Revelation 12:1*), the Lunar goddess and the Apocalyptic Heroine alike personifying the regenerative force, the Sushumna (Living fire), mystically called the World Mother, and described in Card No. 3 of the Tarot as the Empress.

2. Svadhishthana, the prostatic ganglion, was represented by Smyrna, noted for the fig industry. The fig is preeminently a phallic symbol. This is the starting point of the Ida and Pingala Nadis, called the "two witnesses" and also the two golden pipes (which) empty the Golden Oil out of themselves (*Zechariah 4:12; Revelation 11:3*).

3. Manipura, the solar ganglion, was represented by Pergamos, celebrated for its temple of Aesculapius. This is the chief center of the sympathetic nerve system, end the seat of man's epithumetic nature, represented in the Bible by the *Great Red Dragon*, which stood before the woman, who was ready to be delivered, for to devour her child as soon as it was born (*Revelation 12:4*).

This is the Beast, says Hotema in *The Great Red Dragon*, which is devouring you by inches, sapping your vitality, shortening your lifespan, and pushing you into obscurity. You must first conquer this Beast if you would acquire the Secret Power that lifted up to a Higher Level of Consciousness those Masters who gave the world the Ageless Wisdom.

To him who will banish all the animalistic propensities from his own nature, and work his way up to the pure region of Astral Light, "I will give to eat of the hidden Manna, and will give him a White Stone, and in the Stone a new name written, which no man knoweth saving he that received it. And that New Name was not The Word Of God, as falsely recorded in the Bible (*Revelation 19:13*), but the Son of Light. For he was then an Initiate of the Ancient Mysteries, a member of the Great Order of the Ancient Masters, the Children of the Sun, the Order of Melchizedec, the Gospel of which was preached for thousands of years to every creature which is under heaven; whereof I Paul (Apollonius) am made a minister (*Genesis 14:18; Psalms110:4; Hebrews 5:6, 10; 4:17, 21, etc.*)."

4. Anahata, the cardiac ganglion, was represented by Thyatira, a city noted for the manufacture of scarlet dyes; the name being thus a covert reference to the blood vascular system.

5. Vishuidha, the pharyngeal ganglion, was represented by Sardis, a name which suggests the sardion, sardine, or carnelian, a flesh-colored stone, thus alluding to the laryngeal protuberance, commonly called "Adam's apple."

This is the center in the throat which is directly related to the generative centers, as shown by the change of voice at the time of puberty, and the castrato voice of the eunuch.

This is where the biblical makers got their notion of a God who performed the miracles of Creation by speaking the words which produced what he wanted, and giving the world in the first chapter of Genesis a childish story of Creation which ruled all Europe until the 18th century.

6. Ajna, the cavernous ganglion in the center of the forehead, was represented by Philadelphia, a city which was repeatedly destroyed by earthquakes.

The manifestation of the ascending Living Fire at this ganglionic center in the brain is especially violent, and the Bible describes the opening of the sixth seal, which refers to this ganglion, as being accompanied by a "great earthquake" (*Revelation 6:12*)

This cranial center is the Pituitary Gland, the seat of the sixth sense, Premonition, and from him in whom this power is functional at par, the chief captains and bondman hide themselves from his face, and he sitteth on the Throne (*Revelation 6:12-17*).

7. Sahasrare, the conarium ganglion, the Pineal Gland in the Brain, the All-Seeing Eye, was represented by Laodicea, noted for the manufacture of the so called Phrygian Powder, which was

esteemed a sovereign remedy for week or sore eyes, presumably the "eye-salve" mentioned in the Bible (*Revelation 3:14-21*).

When the *Living Fire of Creation*, elaborated and refined at the base of the spine, is conserved and not consumed in masturbation, fornication or procreation, it flows up to the Golden Bowl (*Ecclesiastes 12:6*), and such man sits down with the Father, the Glorious Sun of the Universe, upon the Throne of the God of the whole Earth. He has conquered his animalistic nature, risen to the high level of the angelic plane mentioned in the Bible (*Mark 12:25*), and become truly the Son Of Light (*Revelation 21:7*).

Let us go back and notice again the Order of Melchizedec. This was the very ancient Order of Sun Worshippers, the most sacred and most sublime society of the highest-minded men that the world has ever known, and their Gospel, as Paul said, was preached for thousands of years in all of the lands of the ancient world. It was the Universal Philosophy, but, in time, was perverted and corrupted by the cunning priesthood.

To be accepted for initiation in that ancient Order, the candidate had to prove, by severe mental and physical tests, his worthiness to be entrusted with the secret of the Higher Consciousness which the Masters understood and communicated to the new initiates at the time of their "raising."

Chapter 6
TETRAGRAMMATON

In the Great Mystic Symbolic Tetragrammatons' of the Ancient Masters we have one of their deepest secrets, and there we find the element which formed the basis of the most fraudulent book in all the history of the world. That book, called the Word of God, was compiled by the trickiest set of men that ever united their labor in the art of deception, and no other book on earth has ever done so much harm to humanity as it has done.

In their prolonged study of Created Phenomena, the Masters discovered what they came to call the Sacred Four Elements, as they found that these elements enter into the constitution of everything known. They saw for thousands of years that (1) Soil, (2) Solar Heat, (3) Air and (4) Water are the elements that produce every formation, every object, and every organism.

The Masters then invented an appropriate Symbol to embrace the Sacred Four Elements. That Symbol is known to us as the Sphinx, the image of which has been found in all the lands of the ancient world, and just as far back in the night of time as it is possible for us to go, as related by Professor Hotema in his work titled *The Mysterious Sphinx*.

In his *History of Magic* (1853), the great French Mystic and Kabalist Alphonse Louis Constant, who wrote under the pseudonym of Eliphas Levi, who was always on the edge of excommunication and even worse because of his flaunting of papal authority, and who was called the last of the Great Magicians, mentioned the Sphinx as follows:

"This symbolical tetrad, represented in the Ancient Mysteries by the four forms of the Sphinx, — man, eagle, lion and bull — corresponded with the Four Principal Elements of the Universe, — earth, water, air and fire.

"These four zodiacal signs, with all their analogies, explained the one WORD (of God) hidden in all the sanctuaries (of the ancient world)

.... Moreover, the Secret WORD was never pronounced; it was always spelt, and expressed in four words, which are the sacred words Yod-He-Vau-He."

Of this WORD, Webster's Unabridged Dictionary says: "The Four Consonants forming the Hebrew 'incommunicable name' of the Supreme Being, which in the later Jewish tradition is not pronounced save with the vowels of Adonal or Elohim, so that the true pronunciation is JHVH, JEWH, YHVH, YHWH. Numerous attempts have been made to represent the supposed original form of the word, as Jahaveh, Jahvah, Jahva, Jahveh, Yahve Yahveh, Yahwe, Yahweh, etc."

A lot of nonsense about almost nothing; and badly mistaken are they who believe that this WORD represented the "incommunicable name of the Supreme Being," meaning the church of God of course, and that was known as a fact by the tricky biblical makers. For they knew that WORD represented the Sacred Four Elements in objects and phenomena of quite different categories, between which the man of darkness sees nothing in common, the Initiate saw the analogy between all objects and all phenomena, and was convinced that the Universe and everything in it are constructed and constituted according to the same law and the same design. This was the chief goal of Kaballistic philosophy.

The concept is clear: If the WORD, the Ineffable Name which represents the Four Elements, is in everything, then everything should be analogous to the whole — the atom analogous to the Universe, and all analogous to the WORD, the Ineffable Name, JHVH, "the Word (that) was with God, and the Word was God", says the bible (*John 1:1*).

This knowledge discloses how the Bible came to be called the Word Of God. But it is not exactly the Word of God in the manner in which the deceived masses are taught to think of it.

Confusion vanishes and mystery fades when we are presented with the background of the church God, and the Word of this God, which was very God himself.

In the Word which represented the Sacred Four Elements, we have found only part of the hidden meaning of the Mystic Symbolic

Tetragrammatons. That part which we have found is the external aspect which deals with the Four Elements, Fire, Air, Water and Earth.

A greater mystery is connected with the internal phase of the Symbol, which dealt with the astral aspects that rise as the products of the functions of these Four Elements in the created body of man. These products are another one of the great mysteries of the Universe. They appear as the astral qualities of (1) Vitality, (2) Consciousness, (3) Mind, and (4) Intelligence, and attain their climax in Man, the God of Creation.

Who will analyze their constitution? Most authors who write about Universal Mind and Cosmic Consciousness are wandering in the wilderness.

Mind is a term invented by science and has no concrete meaning. The distinction between Mind and Matter has been the focal point upon which scientists have ERRED FROM THE BEGINNING. They have argued pro and con regarding things in their visible aspects, their appearances, their modus operandi, and have neglected the more important counterparts of these phenomena, viz., and the invisible. Yet, in the realm of the invisible resides the real essence of Matter not only, but of all that exists.

Consciousness is another riddle to science. Harold W. Percival said:

"CONSCIOUSNESS is another mystery, the greatest and most profound of all mysteries. The word Consciousness is unique; it is a coined English word. Its equivalent does not appear in other languages...

"Consciousness is the ultimate, the final Reality. It is that by the presence of which all things are conscious. Mystery of all mysteries; it is beyond comprehension (like the Christian God — Hotema). Without it, nothing can be consciousness; no one could think; no being, no entity, no force, no unit, could perform any function. Yet Consciousness itself performs no function. It does not act in any way; it is a presence, everywhere. And it is because of its presence that all things are conscious in whatever degree they are conscious,

Consciousness is not a cause. It cannot be moved, or used, or in any way affected by anything. It does not increase nor diminish, expand, extend, contract, or change, or vary in any way" (*Thinking & Destiny*, pp. 25-6).

The Consciousness about which this man writes, is unknown to us. We have seen unconscious people, and can render a man unconscious with a blow on the head. There are people who are more conscious than others, and there are insane persons who are Conscious of almost nothing. The evidence proves that Consciousness rises as a function of the brain, the higher is the degree of Consciousness expressed by that person. According to Percival, Consciousness does not increase nor diminish. In that case, all men should manifest the same degree of Consciousness. But they do not.

Much of the teachings of the Ancient Masters centered on man's State of Consciousness, they asserting that man is what his Consciousness is. Such teachings would constitute time and labor if all men possessed the same degree of Consciousness or if Consciousness did not increase nor diminish.

We have said that the Four Astral Qualities expressed by the created body are connected with the internal phase of the Tetragrammaton. They are not Entities but Products, and they spring from the Tree of Life, a mystery of which Percival was unaware. The Tree has its roots deep in the Endocrine Glands, its trunk is the Spinal Cord, its branches are the Nerve System of the body, called the Fiery Man by Professor Hotema in the Flame Divine, and the ruling agency is the Cranial Brain, the Throne of the Most-High Ego, the God Spirit that dwells in the Temple, as stated in the Bible (*1 Corinthians 3:16*).

We are now dealing with Astral Man who is unknown to science and is referred to by science as an Unknowable Reality, these being the exact words used by one of the truly great scientists of modern times, Doctor Alexis Carrel, who said:

"Each man is made up of a procession of phantoms, in the midst of which there strides an Unknowable Reality — Our knowledge of the human body is, in truth, most rudimentary. It is impossible, for the present, to grasp its constitution. We must, then, be content with the scientific observation of our organic and mental activities, and, without any other guide, march forward into the unknown" (*Man The Unknown*, pages 4, 109).

Science and medical art can make little progress in the study of Anthropology, Biology, Psychology, Physiology and Pathology until the nature of the Unknowable Reality, the Astral Tetragrammaton, has been determined. In fact, it is stupid and absurd to talk about progress until we know where we are, where we are going, and why.

Marching forward into the unknown, as stated by Carrel, is a frank admission of facts to prove that science knows but little about Man. The only Science of Man the world has ever had, was that developed by the Atlantean Astrologers over a period of fifty thousand years, and destroyed by the Mother Church in the 4th, 5th, and 6th centuries to hide the true nature of Man and the source of its religious system.

The Sacred Four Elements, Fire, Air, Water and Earth, are the joint-creators not of man, but only of his physical body. This is the point where science gets lost and confusion arises.

Professor Hotema shows in *The Glorious Resurrection,* that the Ancient Masters taught that man is constituted of two bodies, and in the Bible they are termed Terrestrial and Celestial (1 Corinthians 15:40). But science only sneers that assertion and calls it "heathenish superstition," while contemporaneously confessing that man is composed "of a procession of phantoms, in the midst of which there strides an Unknowable Reality," as Carrel said.

Here we have an admission by science of the known existence of an element in man that is a mystery to science, and at the same time science refuses to investigate that mystery in an attempt to determine the constitution of the Unknowable Reality.

The ways of science with respect to man are peculiar and puzzling. The evidence shows on its face that there must be a deep plot to keep man in darkness as to his true nature. And there is a reason for this. If man's true nature were generally known as shown by Prof. Hotema in his work titled *The Soul's Secret*, it would mean the end of religion and of medical art, and the end of the sweetest rackets on earth. This means there'll be no true science of man taught in the schools and colleges as long as religion and medical art can prevent it.

Our purpose here is to do the best we can in determining the true nature of the Four Astral Qualities of man that constitute Carrel's Unknowable Reality.

We have briefly referred to one of them, Consciousness, and observe that it appears as a state of brain function. The same may be said of Mind and Intelligence, for these three qualities instantly vanish when a man is knocked unconscious. Some authorities assert that they are all just the various phases of one state.

The fourth quality, Vitality, seems to be of a somewhat different nature. The unconscious man knows nothing. His Consciousness, Mind and Intelligence, are gone, but he still lives and breathes. This evidence indicates that Vitality depends on some other part of the brain, and research shows that part to be the Medulla Oblongata.

The Medulla is the upper, enlarged portion of the Spinal Cord, being the extension and prolongation of the Cord into the cranium or skull. In the substance of the Medulla are situated the great ganglionic centers which control respiration, deglutition, vomiting, etc. Pressure on the Medulla, and not simple strangulation, is held to be the actual cause of death in the process of judicial hanging.

From the interior portion of the Medulla, and under the surface of the Cerebrum, rise the Cranial Nerves, which emerge from the cranial cavity through openings in the base of the skull. These are distributed to various parts of the head and back, to the organs of special sense, and to some of the thoracic and abdominal organs.

In the posterior and lowest portion of the substance of the Medulla, are located the original source of those certain nerves which indirectly control the organs and functions of respiration.

This is the throne of the Vitality of the body. Living is breathing; and living ends when breathing steps.

And so, we observe that the four astral qualities of Vitality, Consciousness, Mind and Intelligence, are aspects of brain function; that the seat of Vitality, being so important, is better protected from damage than are the rest.

There is a highly important factor involved here that must not be overlooked: While Consciousness, Mind and Intelligence are entirely brain function aspects, vitality is not exactly so. In addition to brain function, there must be suitable air to breathe, or Vitality ends. And Vitality ends quickly if the air one breathes is badly polluted.

In the case of slightly polluted air, the kind that is breathed by man in this civilization from the cradle to the grave, Death creeps on slowly, by imperceptible degrees, as Professor Hotema has explained in detail in his great work titled, *Man's Higher Consciousness*.

And these sinking stages exhibited by the body, as it slowly settles toward the grave, appear as symptoms of distress as the body struggles to live under condition which the great Carrel said made life itself impossible. We quote him here;

"In truth, our civilization, like those preceding it, has created certain conditions of existence which ... render life itself impossible" (page 28).

These are the exact words of one of the greatest doctors of this century. And these symptoms of distress as the body settles toward the grave, are given various names by medical art which mean nothing at all, and are treated by the doctors as though they were actual entities that were attacking the body and trying to destroy it. They are called "disease;" and medical art brags about the "bitter war" it is "waging against disease." Just give us more millions of your dollars for research, says medical art, and we'll rid the world of disease.

If a man desires to increase his State of Consciousness, and rise to the high level where he is able to control, influence or dominate others, he is here learning how that is done. He must first improve the condition of his own body and brain in order to increase his own Consciousness, and that is the secret to which Professor Hotema devoted his attention in his work just mentioned, *Man's Higher Consciousness*. That work should be studied by all who desire better health, longer life, and a higher level of Consciousness.

Chapter 7
Science of Sensology

Due to the limitation of man's organism to receive, register and report relative knowledge, there are states of Force and Matter lying beyond his reach.

In the acquisition of relative Knowledge, man in general has made only limited use of his well-known but little-understood recording devices, his Five Senses, in the quest of observing and examining the nature of Force and Matter in their varying states. This is not his own fault, but that of those by whom he is controlled and governed. Their first task seems to be to keep man's Knowledge limited and keep him in darkness, thus making it easier for them to make him believe what they teach and tell him.

That is another reason why humanity is composed of two classes, (1) intelligent men without religion, and (2) religious men without intelligence.

It would be impossible to make an intelligent man believe the fairy tale, that some God, way off up in the sky somewhere, so loved the world, a tiny speck in space, that he gave his only begotten Son, that whosoever believeth in him should not perish, but have everlasting life (John 3:16).

Science has finally made a great discovery. What is called Matter exists in solid, liquid and gaseous states. And yet these states are only varying degrees of one cosmic substance, universal electricity.

In the changes of solids to liquids, and of liquids to gases, due to the limitation of man's Five Senses, science has had to resort to exact mathematics to become aware of the existence of states of Matter which the Five Senses do not and cannot record.

Science has learned of the existence of states of Matter which the eye cannot see, of colors which the eye cannot distinguish, of sounds which the ear cannot hear, of odors which the nose cannot detect, of flavors which the tongue cannot taste, and, in general, of the existence of solids, liquids, gases and atomic elements which the Five Senses cannot record. In the process of acquiring Knowledge of these various substances, science has finally learned that an exact law of mathematical sequences is operative in all phenomena.

Ages ago the Ancient Masters discovered that all manifestations of relativity are divided into multiples of seven as a fundamental application of natural mathematical law, and that each division of seven again has its seven mathematical variations, and so on ad-infinitum.

By deduction and analogy, the old Masters also accounted for the presence in man of Seven Sense Organs, and determined the possible range of the function of the two extra senses. And what does science do in this field of Higher Knowledge? When any evidence of the existence of these two extra sense powers appears, by accident or chance, scientists promptly dismiss the subject by terming it Intuition, which explains nothing, but does indirectly admit the existence of sensory powers which they cannot analyze.

Here is where the "superstitious heathens" of the ancient world show us something. They located the centers of these two extra sense powers, learned how to activate them, and also determined the approximate extent of their function. And due to the fact that these senses are activated by vibratory manifestations not yet reduced in our system of relative phenomena, this Force has been called Spirit by the religionists.

The Ancient Masters called it Astral Light, a term that means something and is understandable, whereas the term Spirit, invented by the religionists, means nothing, and is not understood even by those who invented it.

As man on the earth plane is a structural pattern of all Creation, we know by deduction and analogy that he is not limited to Five Sense Powers, but possesses Seven.

Yet, what do we know about the Sixth and Seventh Sense Powers? Practically nothing at all. Science even denies their existence. And yet the last book of the Bible deals exclusively, in symbol and parable, with the

Seven Sense Powers of men, — thus revealing how well the secret of these two extra sense powers was known to the Ancient Masters thousands of years ago, and still we call them "superstitious heathens."

The occultists have found that with the Sixth Sense, due to the chemistry of the seven minute organs of that sense-organ-group which are activated by vibrations equivalent to the speed of Light, man is able to receive, translate and transmit vibratory impulses that reverberate, apparently without diminishing force, for thousands of years, through which man can register and repeat any previous set of vibrations sent out over the same instrument, or by voluntary control or adjustment, the vibrations sent out by others which we know as memory in its many phases.

In its negative or receptive phase, the Sixth Sense Organ, the Pituitary gland it the brain, picks up these vibrations and correspondingly activates the entire nerve system of the organism, to give man Knowledge in terms of repeating the impulses of the other Five Senses.

The Seventh Sense Organs, the Pineal gland in the brain, permits direct contact with cosmic vibration in controlled concentrations, and may be regulated to duplicate all vibratory manifestations in Creation, according to cosmic law.

The reader should understand that we are dealing with vibration originally moving at the speed of Light, and reduced in corresponding scales of lower rates reflected in the atomic chart, or being increased by the reverse process.

In the activation of the Seventh Sense Organ, it picks up vibrations which are calculated mathematically to establish speeds of varying degrees, corresponding to the varying degrees of the speed of Light squared.

In its functional state, the Seventh Sense Organ uses the vibrations of the Sixth to attract free atoms and reproduce atomic forms duplicating any phenomenon composed of atoms.

In all this work, occultism accounts for man's functioning on Seven Planes of Existence. However, the mathematics of these Seven Planes indicate the presence of two still higher planes, hence Perfect Man has his source of eternal existence in the Ninth Plane. That being the case, Perfect Man is not subject to Change from any force or combination known to mathematics. In that aspect, Man is Perfect and Eternal as an expression of the Universal Living Fire.

Number Nine

We here discover why Number 9 was of such high importance to the Ancient Masters. They taught that each of the three elements which constitute the human body is ternary: The water element containing earth and fire; the earth element containing igneous and aqueous substance; and the fire element being tempered by globules of fluidal and terrestrial corpuscles which serve to feed it.

None of the three elements being entirely separate from the others, all material objects and bodies are composed of these three elements, whereof each is triple, and may be designated by the figurative number of three times three, which was the ancient symbol of all formations of bodies. Hence the name of the ninth envelope given to Matter.

Every material extension, every circular line, had for its representative sign the No. 9 among the Pythagoreans, who had observed the property which this number possesses of reproducing itself incessantly and entirely in every multiplication; thus offering to the mind of man a very striking symbol of Matter, which is incessantly composed before his eyes, after having passed through thousands of decompositions.

Two times 9 are 18, and 1 and 8 are nine. Three times 9 are 27, and 2 and 7 are nine. Four times 9 are 36, and 3 and 6 are nine. Five times 9 are 45, and 4 and 5 are nine. And so on. In Grecian mythology, Number 9 was consecrated to the Music of the Spheres and to the Nine Muses in Harmony, which refine and polish human nature. They were the Nine Daughters of Jupiter and Mnemosyne (Memory). Each was assigned to preside over one particular department of literature, art or science.

Calliope presided over epic poetry, Clio over history, Euterpe over lyric poetry, Melpomene over tragedy, Terpsichore over choral dance, Polymnia over sacred song, Erato over love poetry, Urania over astrology, and Thalis over comedy.

The 9th Hebrew letter was Teth, one of the simple letters, and was connected with the zodiacal Sign Leo, the heart of the Grand Zodiac Man. The basic meaning of Teth is a serpent, and as 9 was the number of Initiation in the Ancient Mysteries, an Initiate was called a Naga or Serpent of Wisdom (*Genesis 3:1*).

Another reason for the application of this term to the Initiate was, that as the serpent changes and renews its outer skin, so the Initiate changed and renewed his personality; that is, he shook off and emerged from the limitations of the old personality when he became an Initiate. No. 9 also completes and shakes off the old digits, which may be compared to the personality, and emerges in the new number 10.

And just as the newly emerged serpent is the old serpent which has renewed its youth like the eagle's (*Psalms 103:5*), so does the Initiate retain the old, but rejuvenated and youthified, with all the new powers added. For in his long pilgrimage toward the 9th Gate of Life, he has gradually transmuted the old body, and, atom by atom, cast off the seeds of decay, and surmounted the fear of Death by the acquisition of the Higher Knowledge as to its nature, learning that Death is really the gateway to the Future Life, as explained by Professor Hotema in *The Glorious Resurrection*.

The 9th card of the Ancient Tarot is called the Hermit. In it are expressed all the ideas of Initiation; for it presents the picture of an old man who, in spite of the fact that as he walks he leans upon a staff, yet he is vigorous and upright, with glittering eyes, gazing steadily ahead. He is clad in a long Mantle and in his uplifted right hand carries a Lantern, illuminated by the Living Fire of the Interlaced Triangles, the Six Pointed Star, and the Great Symbol of Solomon that reflects Man above as the Man below.

The symbology of this card is clear: The age of the Hermit does not denote senility, but the strength of cosmic maturity, hence experience, discretion and wisdom.

If it were possible to rescue Plan from his lowly, mind-conditioned status in order that he could become aware of his Higher Nature and of the Higher Knowledge, it would be just too bad for despots and religionists, and no one knows that any better than they do. For that man would fear Death no longer, knowing that it is the natural Gateway to the Future Life, as taught by the Ancient Masters in their famous fable of the Crucified God and his Resurrection. For that God is Man, and his Resurrection to the Future Life can occur only through the natural process of the Death of the body.

And we are also learning that at the higher rates of vibration, man is able to transcend the limits of space in incomprehensible fractions of what we call Time. Then knowingly, willfully and by predetermination, he can again manifest as a relative being in other particular environment, or planetary bodies.

In view of what science has determined by mathematical sequences in creative process and cosmic law, scientists have reached the mathematical conclusion that humanoids exactly like us, but closer to our sun and more in line with the source of cosmic radiation, have learned in demonstrated fact what we know in mathematical theory.

This newer Knowledge shows we should not manifest surprise that foreign humanoidal beings, even in great numbers, may visit our planet, and establish appropriate vehicles of transportation, when they contact our atmosphere, and assume grosser physical vehicles of manifestation like our own, to advise and warn us that our stupid violations of cosmic law may destroy all of us, leaving our earth to be re-polluted by other creatures adapted to the new condition. This has happened in the past, when the giant animals of primitive days perished and vanished because of changes in climate and atmosphere to which their organisms were not adapted. Why should it not happen again?

We have already altered the conditions of the atmosphere so that the doctors are finding a constantly increasing number of malformed babies being born, which, or course, means more increase in our downward course of degeneration, which something has already reached the bottom.

Jacques Loeb, the famous investigator, stated that possibly the primal element of Life is so infinitely small, that it may travel on waves of light to other worlds, which appears very feasible.

Thus the Ego, after such a journey, may resume existence in physical form in some other world soon after its release from the body on our earth. On an object measuring one-hundredth thousands of an inch total surface gravitation and light-pressure are equal. Reducing the size still more may entirely free the Ego from gravitation entirely.

Sir Arthur Eddington, in his book *"The Nature of the Physical World,"* estimates that the electrons and protons of a mania body, his flesh, bones and blood, if reduced to a solid mass, would be just visible with a magnifying glass as a tiny speck.

We should ever remember that man is an astral entity as well as a material entity. As a mathematical postulation, no line of demarcation can be drawn between the two; for the material is the astral condensed, as ice is condensed vapor. The terms material and astral, terrestrial and celestial, mean only different degrees of the same phenomena.

Man is constantly seeking greater Knowledge, but fails to use what he already has. To put it more correctly, the Knowledge, is here for which man is searching, but the powers That Be keep him in darkness as to its nature and presence.

Chapter 8
Endocrinology

Man is what his glands make him, says science. But the glands would be life-less and useless without the Nerve System, called the Fiery Man by Professor Hotema in his work titled *The Flame Divine*.

All organs, glands and systems of the body are subsidiary to the Nerve System, through which Astral Light manifests the enigmatical states called Vitality, Consciousness, Mind and Intelligence.

The science of psycho-bio-physiology is based upon the evidence of things unseen. We cannot see light waves, but as they are transformed into nerve impulses and we interpret them, we acquire the evidence of the existence of objects, and say that we see them. That is illusion. What we see is a mental impression of the nerve impulses created by the waves of the objects.

The function of tissues, muscles, organs, glands, and systems of the body is dependent upon the Nerves that supply them with that Cosmic Force which the Ancient Masters called Astral Light and now called Cosmic Radiation. Human beings and the other higher animals seem to be equally favored as to the Nerve System up to the point where the Spinal Cord enters the skull. From there on, man's superior brain development elevates him high above the animal kingdom, exalts him to the angelical level, and he can look down with scorn on the less fortunate lower animals.

But that high state of man does not prevail today. We shall present evidence to show the sad truth, that this Superior Being of the terrestrial plane has gradually declined, through a long process of degeneration, to the point where only a scattering few now occasionally appear who exhibit a degree of intelligence above the law level of the brain-washed, mind-conditioned multitude, who are on a lower level psychically than the beasts of the field and the fowls of the air.

Among the known 25 organs of the body which elaborate, refine and secrete substance necessary for the conservation of its internal equilibrium and the activation of its structures, ten may be considered as the cardinal glands in which we are now interested. These are the thyroid, parathyroid, spleen, pancreas, suprarenal's, thymus, prostate, gonads, pituitary and pineal.

It is well to state in advance that all people in our grand civilization begin to undergo a slow process of degeneration, called aging, that extends from the cradle to the grave, as Professor Hotema has explained in his work titled *Man's Higher Consciousness*; and this condition of degeneration, aging, dying naturally affects every part of the body and all its organs and glands.

And so, the logical result is that there is obviously not one of the endocrine which is not in a state of degeneration, worse in some persons than in others, and the glands involved in the higher functions of the body, the higher Consciousness, are the ones that fade out first and lapse into a dormant or semi-dormant state. There are five of these special ganglionic centers in the body and two in the brain which are of such importance, that the last book of the Bible is devoted exclusively to them, and they are mentioned as Seven Seals because in the average individual they function much below par.

The Book with Seven Seals mentioned in chapter 5 of Revelation is Man's body and the Seven Vital Centers which we have mentioned. The amazing effect on body and mind produced by the normal activation of these seven important ganglionic centers is the remarkable story related in Revelation, in symbol, and allegory, and the student will fine an interpretation of these symbols and allegories in Professor Hotema's Work titled *Son Of Perfection*.

1. Thyroid - Located in the neck, astride of the Adam's apple. It exerts special influence on the general metabolism. While is not built so much like the Pituitary (anabolism), it disintegrates

(catabolism), for it facilitates activity involving the utilization of oxygen in the general exchanges of the body's chemistries.

Many physical disorders result from hypothyroidism (decreased thyroid activity). Those suffering with thyroid difficulties are inclined to be sluggish, indifferent, lack ambition to accomplish and are irritable in disposition. Thyroid inactivity appears more frequently in those past 30 because of greater degeneration.

2. Parathyroid - Next to the Thyroid is closely colonized a quartet of much smaller endocrines, called the Parathyroid Glands because of their proximity to their larger neighbor, two on each side of it. It is the duty of these tiny organs, each about the size of a millet seed, to regulate the amount of calcium in the blood and tissues. They help to maintain a balanced condition of the body, and play an important part in brain, nerve and sex functions.

The Thyroid, Parathyroid, Laryngeal and Pharyngeal regions are ruled by the Vishuddha Chakra, which is the highest of those belonging strictly to the sympathetic nerve system, those above being in the brain. The effects on body and mind of the activation of this ganglionic center are described on body and mind of the activation of this ganglionic center are described in symbol and allegory in verse 8, chapter 6, of Revelation.

3. Spleen - Not considered by some as a ductless gland. It is situated in the left upper quadrant of the abdomen, and is one of the most important filtration stations of the body. It operates under the vibratory control of the Pituitary, "the builder of the Temple," in combination with the Parathyroid, forming an operational Triad.

4. Pancreas - Situated in back of the upper part of the abdomen. It regulates insulin, sugar, starch, alcoholic toxins, etc. It also receives and precipitates minute quantities of niton gas from sunlight or atmospheric gases that have been exposed to sunlight.

5. Suprarenals - A duo gland situated just above the kidneys, the central portion of which regulates adrenalin, the activating fluid of the body, preparing man to flee or fight in the case of danger.

The pounding of the heart, the stronger contraction and more complete evacuation of its chambers, the quickening of the breath, the hair standing on end, the rise in blood pressure, the alteration of the blood so it clots more easily—all that complicated pattern of reaction to a sudden change in the environment which threatens the stability of the organism may be traced to the ubiquitous wires of the sympathetic nerve system as they are affected by adrenalin.

The Pancreas and the Suprarenals are ruled by the Manipura Chakra, located in the Solar Plexus, and its ruling principle is Electric Fire. When the Yogin activates this ganglionic nerve center, known as the Fire Dharana, the killer of the fear of death, then fire cannot harm nor burn the Yogin." — *Kundalini*, page 44.

6. Thymus - More familiarly known as the neck sweetbreads, is situated in the thorax, extending from the throat down to the heart. The gland grows progressively and commensurately with the body as a whole, generally, until the completion of adolescence, after which it gradually atrophies.

Called "The Gland of Youth," medical art says the gland is supposed to disappear gradually as the genital organs develop and become inactive after the age of 21. Like most medical theories, this one is erroneous. A trace of the gland remains all through life, and shows some activity.

Creation is a Master Economist and Constructionist, makes nothing that is not needed, and makes no glands to become atrophied and inactive. There is a definite cause when glands atrophy and lapse into dormancy, and that cause lies in man's unnatural environment and evil habits. For one thing, the unnatural practice of eating cooked and salted food has had much to do in damaging the body and its glands, as Professor Hotema shows in his work, *Man's Higher Consciousness*.

There is mystery about the Thymus that apparently has not been discovered in modern times, but was known to the Ancient Masters. It is true that this gland, as now known, is largest and most active during childhood, but it still functions in adulthood. When we consider that it is not reasonable for any of the glands of the body to atrophy and shrink in size and decline in activity without a definite cause, we are constrained to assume that this condition of the Thymus is unnatural.

It seems here that we are entering the field of generation. In his work titled *The Great Red Dragon,* mentioned in Chapter 12 of Revelation, Professor Hotema says that long ages have passed since parthenogenesis was the regular process of human propagation; and some traces still remain to show the reason why animalistic generation succeeded virginalistic propagation.

Between the ages of puberty and the menopause, it is usual now for woman to expel from each ovary in turn, at monthly intervals, matured ova. This is termed ovulation, and consists in the enlargement of the Graafian Follicle of the ovary.

The enlargement protrudes in the form of a sac filled with fluid and an ovum. Finally, the sac ruptures, and the fluid and ovum flow on to the uterus, and, if fertilized by the male element, the ovum adheres to the uterine wall and develops into an embryo. Otherwise it perishes and is eliminated.

Leading physiologists hold that ovulation, like menstruation, appears as an abnormal condition. It is not usual in the lower female animals, and no reason but degeneration is known why woman should be an exception to the rule. In the days of Moses where were so many non-menstruating women that a special law applied to them, to-wit: "If she be cleansed of her issue, then she shall number to herself seven days, and after that she shall be clean" (*Leviticus 15:28*).

Doctors Shelton and Clements had their famous debate on this subject a quarter of a century ago, titled the Virgin Birth. It was published at the time. Here appears an important point on human development and the Thymus seems to be involved. Experiments show that the gland acts as a "check valve" on the gonad glands. This was markedly indicated in the case of rats. When their Thymus gland was removed, the result was increased sexual activity, greater propagation, faster deterioration, and shorter life. This reveals one cause of humanal degeneration, and, without question, it has been in operation for thousands of years. And that cause is the effect of another cause.

Why do we degenerate and age? Because the endocrines deteriorate and atrophy? And why is this so? There are many reasons and many causes.

Deterioration and atrophy of the Thymus seems to produce that change of puberty, resulting in the atrophy of the male elements in the female, causing excessive development of the female elements at the expense of the male. She declines from Unit to a Semi-Unit.

Science finds that all infants are bisexual in the embryonic stage, but this condition begins to vanish before birth, being succeeded by an unbalanced degree of either maleness of femaleness.

In childhood, the Thymus still appears developed, normal, and functional, showing that Creation always observes perfection as long as it can do so. Then the work of man begins to disturb the balance. And so, it is assumed that in the early days of the race, the Thymus was developed and functional all through life until later crippled by degeneration,

Biologists hold that when atrophy of the Thymus first began, females first appeared as the primary step in the degenerative course. For more data on this point, the student is referred to *The Great Red Dragon* and the Virgin Birth works mentioned above.

Chapter 9
Higher Consciousness

We have now come to the body's glands that are more vitally concerned in the quest of Higher Consciousness, and this subject is so important that they cannot receive too much attention.

7. Prostate - Not definitely regarded as one of the endocrines. Much of its function is still unknown. It lies near the base of the spinal column, is bigger than a hen's egg, contacts the lower portion of the bladder, and through it passes the urethra as it extends from the bladder. It elaborates most of the fluid in which the spermatozoa of the Gonads float, and its rhythmic pulsation during ejaculation in copulation propels the fluid and the spermatozoa into the vagina.

8. Gonads - The Master Glands of the endocrine system. When the function of these glands is better known, it will be understood why the Ancient Masters paid so much attention to Sexuality that they were smeared by their enemies with the term Sex Worshippers. They had no part in the sexual orgies mentioned in ancient history.

The Gonads are the Refining Center of the Living Fire, the Vital Electricity, the Essence of Life, and the Fruit of the Tree which produces his own right.

Long ages of experience prove that Man is the Creator of his own species, and always was. There have been no changes in Universal Law since Man first appeared upon the earth; but we grant, as science suggests, that there may have been some change in the process by which Man is Transformed, not Created, from an Invisible Entity of the celestial world to a Visible Entity in the terrestrial world, as these worlds are designated in the Bible.

The stupid story in the Bible of the creation of Man makes a good fairy tale for children, and that is the exact attitude of the Mother Church in respect to the brainwashed, mind-conditioned masses.

One of the golden secrets of the Ancient Masters is shown by Professor Hotema, in his *Son Of Perfection*, to be connected with the Gonads, and consisted in the conservation of the precious Fruit of the Tree in the center of the Garden, mentioned in the Bible (*Genesis 2:17*).

The student will find a scientific account of the "creation" of Man in Professor Hotema's two works titled *Cosmic Creation* and *Pre-Existence of Man*, and he will find a scientific account of the Future Life in Hotema's works titled *The Soul's Secret* and the *Glorious Resurrection*.

The Gonads are located in the scrotum of the male and in the pelvis of the female. The secretion of the male Gonads consists of active motile spermatozoa, of spermatic granules and of mucus. The latter is secreted by the ducts of the epididymis and the ves deferens, while the Gonads furnish only the spermatozoa, the spermatic granules and a small amount of liquid, just sufficient in quantity to float the spermatozoa of the Gonads into the ducts.

In addition to refining the superior essence that produces a New Person, the Gonads also elaborate glycogen and lactic acid, two of the few substances that stimulate and activate the brain cells, indicating that proper brain function largely depends upon the product of the Gonads, thus partially explaining why insane asylums and the world at large are filled with idiots and imbeciles, who are such because they have dissipated their Vital Essence in masturbation and fornication.

Procreation is the only phase of the function of the Gonads to which science has given attention. This is a serious error. And that function has been condemned all through the Bible. It is condemned in the second chapter of Genesis. It was condemned by Paul in the New Testament (*Romans 7:8-24*). He regarded marriage as the lesser of two evils (*1 Corinthians 7:9*).

The Ancient Masters regarded Procreation as a "destructive" function. It robs the progenitor of the Vital, Creative Essence which is passed on to the progeny. The same law prevails in the vegetal kingdom. It is a Principle of Creation in operation throughout the Living World, known to the Masters thousands of years ago, but not discovered by science until the 20th Century.

In 1937 experiments were conducted in the botanical laboratories of the Indiana University. It was found that "plants keep continuously young by preventing the bearing of offspring," said the report. Professor D. M. Mottier, in explaining the experiments, said, "The results indicated that the plant will not die so long as there is no offspring." The plant under study was the Prothallia of the Ostrich Fern.

Here is the evidence to prove what the Ancient Masters knew and practiced in their work. Procreation is a serious drain on the Creative Essence of the organism. When this drain is prevented, the Creative Essence thus conserved, confers on the body great benefits of the highest order. The individual is exalted to the high level of the biblical angels (*Matthew 22:30*), and such were given a New Name. They were called *The Sons of Light* (*Revelation 19:13*).

We have briefly sketched the intimate relationship existing between the Thyroid and the Gonads. A still higher relationship exists between the Gonads and the Pituitary, the function of the latter being understood so well by the Ancient Masters that it is termed in the Bible, "the builder of the Temple" (*Zechariah 4:6-14*).

The Gonads are controlled largely through the vibratory plane of force of the Pituitary, the chief gland ruling the development of the body, and they are also under the control of the radiant force of the Pineal. Thus, these two glands of the brain, via the Gonads, are in control of all the glands of the body.

One of the most striking examples that can be cited to impress the student of the remarkable effect on the development of the body of the internal secretion of the Gonads, is that which appears in the development of a horse.

No one can look at a pedigreed stallion without admiring, if not actually standing in awe of its splendid physical force, beauty of form and grace and power of action. He is the physical ideal of the horse family.

The physical features one notes as peculiar to the stallion are, first, the great breadth and depth of chest, and great mass of shoulder and hip muscles, the high, arched neck, the fiery eye, and the luxuriant mane and tail. Second, the functional features next noticeable are the greater alertness and constant physical exuberance, as manifested especially in the gait and the frequent whinnying.

The intelligent observer at the horse whew or on the ranch cannot but compare these animals with the gelding. Two colts on a ranch may be full brothers, from the same pedigreed stallion and same pedigreed dam.

At the age of two years these horses may be as alike as two peas in a pod. One of these promising young animals is Chosen to remain unmutilated as a progenitor of its kind. The other is subjected to the veterinarian's knife and deprived of its Gonads. From the day of this operation these two animals, in every respect alike except that one is castrated while the other is not, develop along radically different lines.

Within two years, the stallion develops into the great, fiery-eyed, firm-muscled war horse, such as the General of an Army delights to ride, as he leads his battalions into battle, confident that his horse will carry him right up to the belching mouth of a canon if he wishes to go there. For the stallion is absolutely fearless and tireless.

The gelding, on the other hand, develops into an animal that is in every respect a neuter. Physically, he develops a body almost identical with that of the female of the same species. Temperamentally, he is a patient, plodding beast of burden; and, under good grooming, he may show considerable energy under the control of his driver, who gives him an occasional touch of the whip, he seldom shows any interest in other members of the horse family, either male or female; and in pasture or stable, his neuter gender is ever apparent. While he may contend mildly for a place at the feeding trough, he never essays the defense of any weaker member of the herd; and one stallion would put to flight a hundred like him.

What has made this radical difference in the development and temperament of these two animals? From the beginning of puberty to the appearance of senile decay, the stallion derives remarkable benefit from the refined fluid of the Gonads. This internal secretion is absorbed by the blood and lymph, is carried to the spinal cord, nerve system and brain, to the muscles and the other glands, and that is the reason of the profound difference indicated above. The gelden has been deprived of this internal secretion.

What is true of the horse applies with equal force to man. The young man at puberty begins to receive from his Gonads the internal secretion which leads to the development of his manly powers. The sum total of the qualities peculiar to manhood is called Virility. For the want of a better word, this term has been applied to the male qualities of any animal whatsoever; so that the male qualities of the stallion are also compassed in the term Virility.

An exact parallel of the conditions of the horses described above, can be found in the eunuch. Males who are castrated before puberty, may be described as spineless, namby-pamby molly-coddles, whose temperament manifests the qualities of cringing servitude and lack of initiative.

There is a curious tendency on the part of these people to put on festoons of fat on chest and hips, presenting a pitiable similitude to the general outlines of a woman's figure. These creatures are as different from a virile man as a gelding is from the stallion. The secret of this remarkable difference lies in the fact that they have been deprived of the benefit of the refined Life Essence of the Gonads. While there is some difference, there is not a great deal, in the case of the non-castrated man who dissipates his Life Essence in masturbation and fornication.

Man has the privilege and the knowledge to choose between constructive and destructive practices. But modern civilization and the present code of moral trend to stimulate the Gonads almost continually, seriously depletes the physical and mental level of the race. And if you want to find yourself in prison, just raise your voice in public against it.

The Ancient Masters called the Gonads the Constructive and the Destructive glands, depending, of course, on how they are used. They discovered that the Creative Essence of the glands has a dual purpose. It may be consumed on the low level of animalistic propagation, or conserved to illuminate the Mind and create a higher state of Consciousness. They regarded the Creative Essence as the Living, Conscious, Vital Electricity of the Universe, and taught that it could not be less, since it performs the noble work of Creation in the production of a New Person.

This knowledge proved to be a wonderful discovery. Someday modern science may give it serious attention. This discovery inspired the Masters to write the great allegory concerning the Garden of Eden and the Tree of Life. It constrained them to realize that if the process of procreation be suppressed and restrained, the body and brain are greatly benefitted as a result.

When the Living Fire is not consumed in propagation, masturbation or copulation, it flows up the Spinal Cord, activating, in turn, each one of six vital nerve ganglionic centers above the Gonads listed in Chapter 5, thereby causing these etheric vortices to rotate at terrific speed, and resulting in increased energy to flow into the brain and nerve centers of the body, with the happy results described by Professor Hotema in *Son Of Perfection*.

These amazing results proved the Masters were right. The Vital Electricity invigorated the body and illuminated the Mind, exalting the Masters to such a high level of Consciousness that the world has marveled at their work, which enabled them to discover that the Kingdom of God is not located way up in the sky, but is actually within the human body (*Luke 17:21*).

For the Kingdom of God is not meat and drink, nor a place in space, "but righteousness and peace" (a contented, elevated state of the Mind). And they taught that man is transformed and rises to a higher plane by the renewing (improving) of his Mind, not by believing in a mythical Jesus (*Romans 12:2; 14:17*).

The scope of the world in which man lives depends on the state of his Consciousness. How large would his world be without his Five Senses? How large is his world when he activates the dormant and semi-dormant extrasensory powers termed Premonition and Clairvoyance?

And so, man enlarges his world as he expands his Consciousness; and the expansion depends upon the force of the Living Fire, generated and refined by the Gonads at the base of the spine. When conserved and raised up to the brain, it improves the Mind and increases the Consciousness by activating billions of dormant or semi-dormant brain cells.

It has ever been a known fact that both the impulse and the motive power of propagation of one's own kind, lies in the Progenitals; and that is just as far as science has ever gone in its study of the Master Glands. In fact, science has never seen anything in Sexuality but its relation to man's purpose of propagation on the animalistic plane. To suggest that it has a higher purpose in the individual, and a definite relation to man's State of Consciousness, would do no more than to elicit from our smug science a scornful sneer.

So constantly and consistently has this erroneous opinion been exploited by science, that Sexuality has never yet been analyzed, as a principle, to modern intelligence. It has been taught by science in its physical functional capacity only, and its higher, psychical function is utterly unknown to science. This is a serious error of science which is reflected back upon society through false literary and social doctrines, involving sexual questions and relations.

The Ancient Masters who have been disparagingly called Sex Worshippers, discovered in their long researches, that Sexuality is much more than a purely physical function. They found that it plays a higher role in man's life than the mere perpetuating of the species. They saw in Life more than feeding and breeding, and they opined that Men has a nobler destiny in store for him than that advocated by the despots and religionists, of rearing the largest number of progeny, to be used as soldiers by the despots and as slaves by the priesthood.

When he visited India about 45 A.D. to study the Hindu Religious System, Apollonius, the eminent Pythagorean Philosopher, the great man of his time in Asia Minor, who became the God of the natives, the Jesus of the Bible, the Paul of the Epistles, and the John of Revelation, was informed by the Hindu doctors that for thousands of years they had known of the exceptional value of the Gonads, and had been grinding up dried Gonads into powder, which they gave to their parents in their work of improving the body and restoring its vigor.

These doctors knew ages ago what we are just learning. They knew that dynamic vitality derives most of its force from the Kundalini Fire produced by the Gonads, and yet medical art appears to know almost nothing of it. Men and doctors go right on wasting the most precious fluid of the body in masturbation, copulation and propagation.

The Prostate and Gonads are ruled by the Svadhishthana and Muladhara Chakras mentioned in Chapter 5, and the effects on body and Mind of the activation of these ganglionic centers are described in symbol and allegory in verses 2 and 12-17 of the 6th chapter of the last book of the Bible, which was originally compiled by Apollonius, long before the world ever heard of the gospel Jesus, from a precious Hindu Scroll given him when he visited India as mentioned above.

The student should read the history of this wonderful man as related by Professor Hotema in his work titled *Mystery Man of the Bible*.

Chapter 10
Teleology

When man invented the radiophone and television mechanisms, he was proud of his accomplishments. He had moved deeper into the darkness of the invisible world, which science stubbornly claims does not exist.

As man copies the mysteries of Creation, it aids us in understanding the functions of the various glands of the body. Some glands perform these functions, but in a much higher degree than man's inventions, as demonstrated by birds and beasts, mentioned in Chapter No. 3.

In referring to these Higher Powers of Consciousness, the great scientist of this century, Doctor Alexis Carrel, said:

"The existence of finality within the organism is undeniable. Each part (of the organism) seems to know the present and future needs of the whole, and acts accordingly.

"The significance of Time and Space is not the same for our tissues as for our Mind (Note: The big question is, Why not? The body is a Unit and the Mind, organs, glands and tissues are all intimately connected and related — Hotema.)

"The body perceives the remote as well as the near, the future as well as the present (Note: Evidence appears in ancient records showing that the Ancient Masters possessed these extrasensory powers, and were called Seer — Hotema).

"The teleological correlation of organic processes is evident in the regeneration of blood after a hemorrhage — Individual cells (in the body) appear to act in the interest of the whole, just as bees work for the good of the hive. They seem to know the future, and they prepare for it by anticipated changes in their structure and function' (*Man the Unknown*).

More than thirty years ago Doctor G.R. Clements presented similar evidence in these words:

"The body is not a finished product with variant and definite limitations, but a living process with almost infinite possibilities. There is a Prevision and a Provision within the living organism by which it may rise superior to environment as well as to heredity, until it meets and masters the condition of a progressive or an established achievement.

"The Prevision is the power to visualize and realize the ultimate effect of the unnatural use of any substance, and guard against this effect by vigorous reaction, yielding to the inimical influence through the Power of Vital Adjustment only when the primary reaction is disregarded, as the smoker who persists even after the first smoke made him sick.

"The Provision is the power of selective adaptation, which is operative not along in the conscious, but also in the unconscious region. Adaptation involves selection, and the power of selection places the organism on the plane of Mind. The ultimate act of Mind is the appropriation or rejection of the present materials of supply. Appropriation is in order to assimilation, and implies the qualities of intelligence, sensation, and volition, represented by three points of the Solar Cross of the Masters. Tejection is in order of self-preservation, and implies the same qualities.

"The living organism is, therefore, self-conserving in the highest degree. There is reason and purpose in all of its structures and functions, and these are created and designed to accomplish specific results. The wise doctor opines that all organized bodies exist as such by virtue of a final cause; that purpose alone rules supreme as the law governing all processes in organic Nature; that in organized bodies nothing is in vain. Not to know the law nor the purpose of function of an organ, does not subvert the facts, nor make necessary or legitimate any procedure contrary to the facts" (*Law of Life & Health*, 1926).

Now we shall notice the glands chiefly responsible for "The existence of finality within the organism," as stated by Carrel. There are two of the body's glands that are the leaders in this respect. They are located in the brain and are called the Pituitary and the Pineal. Science has discovered some of the remarkable functions of the former, but knows almost nothing about the functions of the latter.

9. Pituitary - Located in the front part of the brain, between the top of the ears, in a closely fitting bony Chamber, within the skull. This tiny chamber was poetically designated the Sella Turcica, or Turkish saddle, by its first describers in modern times, the metaphor suggested by the bony flares of its sides. The third ventricle of the brain extends into the stem (infundibulum) and the rear of the gland. The occultists assert that the rear part is the Throne of Astral Man, and the front part is the Throne of the Psychic Body which controls the involuntary functions of the body.

The gland has two lobes, the anterior lobe regulating the chemistry of growth maturation, and sexuality, producing several important hormones. The posterior lobe regulates the fluid content of the body, contracts the muscles, governs blood pressure, urine flow, excretion of milk, etc.

If the secretion of the anterior lobe is diminished during childhood, disproportions of the skeletal development occur. If the secretion is increased, the results will differ, depending on the time in life at which this appears. Should it be manifested during puberty, the figure of the circus giant results.

All of these variations in functions of the gland were known to the Masters, and in the Bible, 4th chapter of Zechariah, appears an interesting fable relating to this gland, there symbolized as Zerubbabel, the builder of the temple (human body).

The Pituitary is also the region of the Ajna Chakra, the central area between and just above the eyebrows, where the head of a Serpent protrudes in the picture of the Egyptian Masters, indicating the activation of the Sixth Sense, and showing they were aware of this superior state of Consciousness.

Rishi Singh Gherwal wrote: "The Ajna Chakra is the source of all Sidhis. (The Living Fire) reaching here, the Yogi controls all the finer forces of the body. He rises above the cosmic elements and is one with Atma, above the world's miseries. His mind listening to the inner soul of the Nada — it is the joy that can be known only by him who has attained this (conscious) state" (*Kundalini*, page 78).

The effects on body and mind of the activation of this great nerve plexus are described in symbol and allegory in the 9th, 10th, and 11th verses of chapter 6 of Revelation interpreted by Professor Hotema in *Son Of Perfection*. The clergy know nothing about these psycho-bio-physiological processes, thinking the book of Revelation refers to God and Heaven.

If all the facts were known, they would show that all the discussion about God and Heaven in the Bible was never copied from the Ancient Scrolls, but are fraudulent interpolations of the biblical makers.

Another important function of the Pituitary is its powerful influence on the rebuilding and repairing functions of the body through its control of the actions and reactions of the other glands and organs, whose duty it is to build, repair and revitalize the organism as a whole.

Chapter 11
Seership

Revelation is the great book of the Bible. It covers in fabulous form the well-guarded secret of Personal Power, and the fable has been interpreted by Professor Hotema in *Son Of Perfection*. The story describes in deep symbol and allegory the psychic emotions and physical sensations experienced by the Neophyte when initiated in the Ancient Mysteries and his Higher Powers of Consciousness were awakened.

That Neophyte in this case was Apollonius, the great Pythagorean Philosopher of the first century. He wrote the fable some two-hundred-fifty years before the world ever heard of the gospel Jesus, which means, of course, that all references to this Jesus are fraudulent interpolations of the biblical makers.

What is the basic source of Personal Power? The great Kingdom Within. Man is what his Consciousness is, consequently Consciousness becomes the pivotal point of our discussion. What Consciousness is and its source are big questions which science has never been able to answer. Experience shows that Consciousness is not a stable, changeless entity, as most authorities believe. If it were, it could not be increased nor decreased, and could never be absent while man is alive. And yet a man may be unconscious, devoid of all Consciousness, and know nothing at all for days and weeks, and still be alive.

Research by leading scientists disclose that Consciousness is a product of man's brain, nerves and glands. That makes these structures highly sacred parts of the body, and they were so revered from all antiquity, and symbolized again and again in all philosophies and religions of the world.

The Ancient Masters discovered that they could increase their Consciousness by improving their brain, nerve system and glands. Modern literature on this subject is practically nil. And there is a good reason. Masters can't be enslaved therefore Masters are not wanted.

The nerve system is dual, but functions as a unit. It is composed of (1) the cerebro-spinal system, consisting of brain and spinal cord, and (2) the sympathetic or ganglionic system, consisting of a series of ganglia, which are small centers of vascular neurine, strung along each side of the spine, from the head down to the coccyx.

The cerebra-spinal system may be termed the extrinsic system, in that its major function consists of keeping man aware of the external world and the adjustment of his organism to extraneous influences.

The sympathetic system deserves the term intrinsic, as it rules and regulates the automatic functions of major importance within the body proper. It is the adjustment system by means of which function and disturbances of function within the body are maintained at a proper balance in their relation the one to the others. For instance, if one organ is getting too much blood and another too little, the sympathetic system promptly makes due adjustment for the proper balance of such conditions.

In analyzing the psycho-bio-physiological processes that produce and regulate man's Consciousness, we must consider the ganglia of the sympathetic system and the forces associated with them. Due to a paucity of literature on this vital subject, in spite of millions of dollars spent in medical research, we must go back for the data we want to the ancient Upanishads of the "superstitious heathens." Therein we find man's psychic nature more fully elucidated than in any other literature available. For in those ancient days the vital knowledge of Life and Man was not concealed as it has been since the Mother Church was founded in the 4th century. Today even the better doctors are unable to analyze the great mystery of Life.

Doctor Robert A. Millikan, world renowned scientist, head of the California Institute of Technology, authority on Cosmic Rays, said "I cannot explain why I am alive rather than dead. Physiologists can tell me much about the mechanical and chemical processes of my body, but they cannot say why I am alive" (Collier's, Oct. 24, 1925).

Scientists are in that dark state of ignorance as to Life because they refuse or fail to recognize the existence of the element which causes a grain of corn to grow, when planted, and reproduce itself.

In those very ancient scriptures of the "superstitious heathens", these ganglia are called Chakras, meaning disks or wheels, and we are told that they revolve with terrific speed. Forty-nine of them are counted, of which Five Key Centers appear along the spine, and two in the head. These are listed in Chapter 5 of this work.

When seen clairvoyantly, the Chakras resemble electric sparks. Each of the Seven has six of lesser importance surrounding it, thus forming six pointed stars diagrammatically, but in the body the centers are not arranged in star-like order. Of the Seven Chakras, the Conarium or Pineal Gland in the brain is the one chiefly concerned in the Higher Consciousness. It closes and fills the gap in the Universal Link between the Microcosm and the Macrocosm, binding the Created to the Creator as stated by Professor Hotema in *The Flame Divine*.

Through this channel, Cosmic Consciousness, as Astral Light, flows from the Astral Realm into physical man, and in him becomes individualized on the terrestrial plane. But the function of the Pineal in this work depends upon the activity of the other Six Key Centers, and largely upon the Ajna or Cavernous Plexus. It requires the Living Fire from the base of the spine to activate the Pineal in this work. As the arc of that Fire, from the Ajna Chakra, contacts the Pineal, phenomena occur which are quite startling to the Neophyte. These phenomena include flashes of temporary Clairvoyance, exhibited by certain persons.

The work of making these two centers of Higher Consciousness function together constantly, requires a career consecrated to the highest development of psycho-biophysiological living and training. That was the goal of the Ancient Masters. Reading books to learn how to live the higher life is one things, but leading a life that lifts you up above the common level of the brain-washed, mind-conditioned masses is another.

It must be done in secret. It cannot be done publicly, for you are outlawed, ostracized, and condemned if you fail to conform and refuse to live in harmony with the orthodox social patter. And the misled multitude that believes the ruling institutions of the land are working for the good and betterment of humanity, ask why the Masters don't show themselves and publically teach the secrets of the Higher Consciousness. There is an old saying that when the student is prepared and ready, the teacher appears.

10. Pineal - The most peculiar, most mysterious and most celebrated of all the body's glands. Anatomically, it is a small, dark-red, acorn-shaped structure, attached by a tiny stalk to the rear boundary of the wonderful, fluid-filled cleft in the brain, termed the third ventricle, which holds the geography of the Throne of the emotions and instincts, and the metabolic centers related to them, according to science.

The first information we find is the fact, that this marvelous gland is now considered by science as useless in man. It is assumed by modern anatomists to be the vestige of an atrophied eye, and hence is termed by them the "unpaired eye." They even assert that the Pineal is supposed to begin to atrophy in man at about the age of seven years, but "this involution is not really complete until puberty," says one authority.

And so we learn that, under our gay way of Life, the most important gland in the entire body begins to waste away at the early age of seven years, and at puberty it has atrophied to the stage where it becomes a "rudimentary structure" regarded as of no value to man in his present stage of evolution, according to science. If that type of evolution can continue long enough, man himself will disappear along with his glands.

But adds science, "in certain vertebrates it attains a much higher degree of development than it does in man." And why not? We should understand that Creation makes nothing in vain, and the present vestigial structures appearing in the human body are the remnants of organs and glands that were once developed and functional before man had suffered the degree of degeneration that now afflicts the race.

That "much higher degree of development" of this important gland in the lower animals, accounts for the mysterious state of Higher Consciousness, exhibited by them, which our smug science brushes off with little notice under the meaningless term Instinct.

"In the lamprey, lizard, etc.," say science, "it (the Pineal) is present in the farm of the so-called Pineal Eye. In structure its resembles, in these animals, an invertebrate eye, and it possesses a long stalk, in which nerve-fibers are developed. Further, it is carried through an aperture in the cranial wall, and consequently lies close to the surface of the dorsum of the head between the parietal bones" (Cunningham's *Text Book of Anatomy,* page 612).

The better development of the Pineal in the lower animals is, without doubt, the inexplicable reason why migratory fowls can fly great distances in the fall without a compass to guide them, over hundreds of miles of open ocean, directly to a friendly region in the south, which Instinct tells them is their proper place of safety from the killing blizzards that grip the frozen land of ice and snow, often bringing death to hundreds of people in one season who are not guided by the Wisdom of the birds.

And these fowls know, by Instinct, when it is time for them to return to the north in the spring, which they do regularly, and usually via entirely different routes, to the exact spots from which they departed months before. Uncanny but true.

Science regards this display of Higher Consciousness so lightly, that it makes no definite attempt to determine the reason of it. That sort of research presents no apparent pecuniary possibilities, hence science is not interests.

In their researches of the 19th century, biologists found that in certain reptilian creatures, currently exemplified by certain lizards, the Pineal is associated with the presence of retinal tissue, and so may-have once functioned as a third or Cyclopean eye as well as a gland.

This fact constrains some to say that we have discovered the Single Eye referred to in the Bible, which fills the "whole body full of light" (*Matthew 6:22*).

Rene Descartes, the mathematical philosopher who said, "I think, therefore I am," conferred upon the Pineal the high distinction of being the mechanical center of the play of forces in the cranium, and hence decided that it was the locus of the abode of the Immortal Ego. And that important gland begins to atrophy in modern man at the tender age of seven years.

It is logical to assert that if man were equipped with the normal glands which he once had, he'd be the wonder of the age. For he'd rise far above the present level of Consciousness, provided of course that he did not become, like he now is, a trustful victim of the sordid institutions engaged in the work of brain-washing and mind-conditioning, and do it so slyly that modern man believes these institutions are interested in his betterment and enlightenment. That is another reason why man's state of Consciousness is at such a low ebb.

To modern science, the Pineal and its functions are a mystery. It is known that when it becomes disordered in children, practically always males, the child becomes affected by a striking sexual and sometimes intellectual precocity. The child develops suddenly, overnight as it were, the sexual organs enlarge and become active, and a rental agility and maturity may be displayed far beyond the years of the individual. And his decline is almost as sudden. He ages rapidly and has a short life. That is part of the answer to the question, 'Why do we age?'

Science has found that extracts of the Pineal, injected into successive generations of animals, will produce sexual precocity, with a concomitant retardation of growth, for growth and sexuality are antagonistic. As sexual function is the process of Creation that cares into action for the purpose of preserving the species before the individual producer goes to the grave. It may be called the last-minute effort of Creation to produce while there is yet time.

These animals, subjected to the injection of extracts of the Pineal, are in fact the most fantastic dwarfs ever experimentally produced in the laboratory. Rats the size of one's thumb have been produced, with broad face and round head, bulging eyes and short snouts. Altogether, these Pineal Produced Dwarf Freaks confirm completely the conclusions drawn by clinicians years ago, concerning the influence of the Pineal in the functional balance of the organs of the body.

We are told that the Pineal is directly responsible for memory, expectation and anticipation. Little wonder that most men have such poor memories and so little expectation and anticipation. We are further told that if it were not for the Pineal, we'd have no knowledge of the past or the future. Most of the mind-conditioned masses have very little now, and will never have more so long as it can be prevented by the institutions which rule our civilization.

Man with his atrophied glands and deficient Consciousness cannot improve his condition by attuning himself to the Wisdom of the Ages, as recommended in the advertisements of the big book-sellers. That man cannot grasp the inner power of his Mind when his glands, responsible for Mind and Memory, are atrophied and defective.

The ancient Hindus regarded the Pineal as the seat of the psychic faculties, the capacities of intuition and supersensory wisdom, which certain oddly "gifted" persons display. The appearance of being oddly "gifted" indicates a better condition of their endocrine glands. And why do these oddly "gifted" persons sink to the common level in time? Because of a mode of living that produces degeneration of the whole body, including the glands.

It has been found that deep concentration stimulates the Pineal if its atrophy has not gone too far. The more we black out our Consciousness by concentration, the deeper we move into the subconscious department of the Mind.

We are told that only one-tenth part of the Mind is conscious, the balance being subconscious. By deep concentration, we voluntarily increase the scope of our Consciousness by drawing from the subconscious department.

This may be accepted as the esoteric meaning of the advice in the Bible, to enter into thy closet when thou prayest (*Matthew 6:6*). And prayer should always be directed to a deep desire for more knowledge of how to use what we already have, and never to asking for more of anything — but Knowledge. Determine to make better use of what we have, and to improve ourselves, is the Royal Road to Success.

We are not bound and limited when we knowingly grasp the depth of the great Law of Infinity. Then we realize that our own higher development depends entirely upon our own well-directed efforts, not upon receiving more from some external source, but upon better development of what we already have, of the whole Kingdom of God within. That means all. Where shall we search for more?

There is no more. The body has all it needs. Everything in the Universe is represented in the body itself. But much of what the body has is in a serious state of degeneration due to the fact that man reaps as he sows (*Colossians 6:7*). This degenerate condition is not improved by asking in prayer for more of anything except KNOWLEDGE AND UNDERSTANDING (*Psalms 119:34*).

The Bible wisely says to ask the beasts, and they shall teach thee; and the fowls of the air, and they shall tell thee (*Job 12:7*).

Go not to those engaged in the task of brain-washing and mind-conditioning, erroneously called education; but go to the bugs and the birds, who are guided by the law of the Universe, and which knowledge appears in the lower animals as Instinct. Let them tell and teach you how to live in order to improve and make better use of what you have.

Remember that nothing weakens man more than dependence upon external aid. And nothing damages the body more and cripples the precious glans worse than the vile products of commercialism and the poisonous concoctions of the doctors, as explained by Professor Hotema in his work titled *Why Do We Age*.

Chapter 12
Astral Light

The last book of the Bible is a wonderful fable. It describes in symbol and allegory the psychical sensations and physical emotions experienced by the Neophyte during his initiation in the Egyptian Mysteries in the Great Pyramid Temple.

This particular Neophyte was Apollonius, the great Pythagorean Philosopher of the first century, from whose voluminous writings the New Testament was compiled. He proved his worthiness to become an Initiate by hanging on a Cross until he was unconscious. Such a man would never reveal the Sacred Arcane of the Ancient Masters through fear of torture. It was he who wrote that fable, and, after his demise at the age of 98, he was worshipped as a god by the people of Asia Minor.

In tracing down the stories and statements in the New Testament, it is found that every one of them is an embellished, magnified, exaggerated, fraudulent account of events which actually happened. And this knowledge reveals why the ancient scrolls and libraries were burned by the Mother Church. Consider how simple it was to change this actual Cross Experience of Apollonius to the fraudulent Crucifixion Story of Jesus.

The great scientist, Doctor Alexis Carrel, considered man a god, and said, "Man stands above all things. Should he degenerate, the beauty of civilization, and even the grandeur of the physical universe, would vanish" (*Man The Unknown*, Pref. page xiv).

Doctor Arthur A. Beale of London, referred to Man as "The Living God," mentioned the vanishment of the old materialism in science and the rabid dogmatism in religion.

This change represents the passage of man from the darkness of the fanatical religionists, which enveloped all Europe for more than a thousand years, to the Light of Universal Law, Common sense and Reason of modern times.

When we contemplate the beauty, complexity, mystery and perfection of the human body as a Temple, incorporating and including all the cosmic forces operating in the Universe, microcosmic in size and extent, involving various systems of operation and action, each more or less complete and sufficient in itself, yet working jointly, and all these numerous systems intermingled, blended and built into one another, and correlated so as to form a Grand Unit of activity, we are overwhelmed with stupendous wonderment.

There is a perfect system of motors in the muscles of the body, a perfect wiring system in the nerves for outflowing conduction, a multiplicity of condensers and transformers, large and small, even representatives in each cell action, resulting in grades of higher and lower tension according to the requirements of the body.

The circulation of nervo-electro-motive force can be tested and proved by delicate galvanometers, producing evidence of a circulation ultimately flowing out into the air in spite of a perfect insulation system of skin. In the higher cerebral departments, the cortex or surfaces of the cerebrum and cerebellum, are the terminal dendrons, acting as aerials conducting by a wireless system, waves to and from the brain, to and from the higher mental centers outside the brain in the psychic auras, the invisible part of man's constitution.

Herein we are able to link up an invisible, transcendental mentality, functioning in its own super-etheric realm, in one of the higher astral encasements of the human entity, corresponding in man to the Astral Light of the Universe, one layer of which registers as the subconscious memory, all the activities flowing from the body.

The Ancient Masters discovered that Astral Light holds the memory of its activities which can be, and are, tapped by certain psychic and sensitive, clairvoyants, and clairaudients. That is another reason why Astral Light, currently called Cosmic Radiation, was so highly esteemed by the Masters, who said that is quaternary qualities, heating, cooling, dissolving and coagulating, when directed by man's will, can modify all phases of natural phenomena, producing life or death, love or hatred, wealth or poverty, in accordance with the given impulsion.

The body presents various degrees of tenuous structure, starting from grossly physical, with clear cut form, varying in different persons according to size and shape. And the Masters knew that behind and beyond, both in extent and subtlety of substance, there exists a ghostly replica which persists after the demise of the physical body, and can be seen by certain sensitive and clairvoyants, especially in cemeteries, hovering over the graves of the decedents. The Hindus regarded this as the Astral Body, the Model, and the Archeus, which is described by Professor Hotema in *Pre-Existence Of Man.*

Everything known to us in the human body and visible from the outside, has a corresponding astral replica, identical in shape but ethereal in structure, and hence invisible to our physical sight.

There is blended in man, a compound of all the various kingdoms of the Universe. In his brain are functions part physical, part astral, and part mental. The brain itself is a mighty switchboard that receives vibrations from above the super sensuous realm, and from below from sensuous realms in the body, transmitting them in both directions; the upper as a direct, controlling, inspiring creative force; and the lower as a flow of experience, impressions, lessons, that are transmitted to those supersensitive states of astralistic, as a record of all the events that happen; the whole system representing a dual circulation, (a) the circulation of the grand cosmos, and (b) the cosmos of man.

From the cranial switchboard in the head, the system is continued down into the body by vital electro-magnetic waves, called nerve impulses, to nerve plexuses which are receiving stations, and where directions are changed.

Then there is the wonderful system of synapses where the nerve fibrils or dendrons terminate, and hook up with others by an electrical arrangement of opposing fibrils, where the currents of vibration are transmitted over a gap by a process ad induction, as in an induction coil.

In Chapter 11 we mentioned two nerve systems. Most of the electric currents from the brain are sent down the spinal cord, from which they are distributed to the body by the nerves, the conveyers of messages from and to the brain; the efferent nerves belonging to the motor department and the afferent to the sensory. This combination is called the cerebra-spinal nerve system.

The other nerve system, separate from but working in perfect harmony with it, is the sympathetic system, which rules the automatic actions, controlling the vital organs, respiration, circulation, digestion, defecation, assimilation, elimination, etc.

Man's Mind that great mystery to science, rises from the action of Astral Light on certain brain centers created for that purpose, and, in order to contact safely our vital organs, the powerful Astral lights requires a process of "stepping down," similar to voltaic current of regular electricity that is transformed to meet the requirements of a small motor.

Such transformation is the task of the psycho-mental apparatus, the agent or downward projection of the Ego. This is the individual, intellectual or brain-mind, and resides in, or is invested in, the astral part of man not exactly in the brain but in direct contact with the brain, and working through it by a connection with the wonderful Pineal Gland. In other words, Astral Light is the active force and the brain and its organs are the instruments which respond.

The Pineal has direct connection with the Pituitary as we have seen, and the latter, the recognized hierarchy of the endocrines, is constituted to receive and transmute the current of Astral Light into those elements that are suitable for the other endocrines on a lower level of psycho-physico-physiological function.

The next station of transformation is the Thyroid, and so on through the entire endocrine system, each gland performing its allotted part and constituted to do its work perfectly. But the present degenerate state of the human body reflects the sad state of its vital organs and glands, and surprises us to see that it does so well and lives as long.

We have seen that from all the endocrines there are emitted the elements called hormones, which enter the blood and lymph, pass through the body in a complicated peregrination and interaction, thus stimulating and activating the various endocrines according to their constitutions.

We think little of the common process by which light is made to flow from a globe when powered by an electric wire. But we are astounded when told that Consciousness flows from the brain when powered by Astral Light. And yet man is the imitator while Cosmic Creation is the Originator.

Man had constituted the globe to produce the element called light, and the Ancient Masters discovered that Creation can make organ that produce Consciousness Mind and Intelligence.

In this Chapter we are presenting additional data concerning those mysterious qualities of men which puzzle science. The student is informed that Consciousness rises from a transformation of Astral Light by the endocrines of the body, which are made for that purpose. And the brain is not Mind nor Consciousness, but a switchboard through which Astral Light makes Man aware of his own existence and of the world in which he lives.

Astral Light is another name for Cosmic Electricity, the greatest and most universal power known. It is this electro-magnetic force which the religionists, in bewilderment, foolishly call God. Then they forget in time how they got their God, bow down and worship their Idol, and even claim that for their idolic God nothing is impossible.

Man, the clever imitator, regards it as a common event now to make radios and television sets that respond to cosmic radiation and bring him messages and pictures from all over the world. For millions of years Creation, the Grand Originator, has been making instruments that respond to cosmic radiation and has covered the earth with them.

Creation makes a body and equips it with organs and glands for the definite purpose of operating as an instrument, when powered by Astral Light, to produce Vitality, Consciousness, Mind and Intellect. It is highly inconsistent to reject that statement as absurd, in view of what we know by experience that man, the clever imitator, can do.

But science adopts that very course. It pities as ignorant those who make such assertions, while it has sought for a century, and in vain, to solve the riddle of Life and Consciousness on the basis of physics and chemistry. Its field of physics and chemistry is littered with unsolved problems, and its weakness to explain anything basic in matters of biology and psychology is extreme. It could hardly be worse.

Referring to this ignorance of science, the great Doctor Alexis Carrel exclaimed: "The illusions of the mechanists of the nineteenth century, the dogmas of Jacques Loeb, the childish physico-chemical conceptions of the human being, in which so many physiologists and physicians still believe, have to be definitely abandoned" because time and experience prove they are erroneous (*Man The Unknown*, page 108).

In all of its orderly operations, Creation presents an eternal pattern that remains fixed and permanent. It never varies nor changes. To form a comprehensive understanding of the innumerable phases of the processes, makes it necessary to strain to its utmost, the greatest human intellect. Even then it becomes apparent that the countless operations which occur are so varied, that only a small percentage of them can ever come under direct observation; and even these which do are the lesser important ones, as the greater take places in the astral realm of the unseen.

Had we been told forty or fifty years ago about the electrified state of the atmosphere surrounding the earth, which we accept today as a proven fact, of course we had refused to believe it.

And there is evidence in the ancient scriptures which shows that the Ancient Masters knew all this, but that evidence was not understood by us until our recent discoveries in the field of Astral Light, Cosmic Electricity, or Cosmic Radiation. Call it what you like.

We realize now that we do live, and move, and have our being in a seething sea of electrification. And this Electrified Sea is the Living Fire which the Bible calls God. "For our God is a Consuming Fire" (*Hebrews 12:29, etc.*).

Therefore, if we accept as God the Living Fire of the Universe, then we have embraced the Almighty God of the Ancient Masters, and not the anthropomorphic God of the blind religionists.

Chapter 13
The Living Fire

The Bible says, "Our God is a Consuming Fire" (*Hebrews 12; 29, etc.*).

"Fire is the perfect and unadulterated reflection of the Cosmic Flame. It is Life and Death, the Origin and the End of every material thing known. It is Divine Substance." — Blavatsky, Secret Doc. I, 146.

"The Essence of the Divine Ego is Pure Flame, an Entity to which nothing can be added and from which nothing can be taken" (Curtiss, *Key Of The Universe*, page 263).

'Fire Philosophy is the foundation of all religions — Without Fire and the resultant heat, there could be no existence — The whole round of peculiar emblems which so puzzle antiquarians, and which are found in all countries, point to the ancient belief in Fire as the First Principle" (Clymer, in *Philosopher Of Fire*).

We devoted much of Chapter 11 to a discussion of Astral Light, the Universal Power which may be called Cosmic Radiation, Cosmic Electricity, Pure Flame, Cosmic Flame, or Living Fire. Due to its high importance, we shall give the subject more attention here.

In *Cosmic Creation* Professor Hotema shows that Fire transforms all elements into one Universal Substance, called Incandescent Gas, the First Principle, the Universal Element which contains in itself everything, and which produces of itself everything, making every object and every organism the product of Condensed Incandescent Gas.

This summarily presents in pointed terms the mystery of the One Universe, the One Principle, the One Substance, the One Power, and the One Law, all of which combined the religionists stupidly call God. Much too simple for science, much too profound for religionists, much too complex for evolutionists, and much too abstruse for laymen.

The Living Fire makes everything and does everything known and unknown. It is Creator and Vitalizor. It makes man and animates his frame. It forms his brain, organs and glands as specific agencies through which to manifest Vitality, Constitution, Mind and Intellect, the quaternary qualities of man which are such an enigma to science.

The Universal Power so great that it can do all things, that it can create a New Person, and that the scope of its work and the extent of its operations are unlimited is certain to perform marvelous mysteries when conserved in the body and not consumed in masturbation, copulation and procreation.

The student will appreciate more the weight of this assertion by reviewing what we said in Chapter 9 about the remarkable difference that develops in two male horses when nothing more is done to one of them than removing the gonad glands.

The higher functions of the body produced by the Living Fire when it is conserved and refined by the gonads, was one of the profound mysteries to which the Masters devoted so much attention, that their enemies smeared them with the term Sex Worshippers; and this epithet has been greatly magnified and exaggerated through the centuries by the Church, in its constant campaign to discredit the work of these Wise Men, whose scriptures it stole and distorted to make its Bible.

When this Universal Power is conserved as stated, it then flows up the Spinal Cord to the Brain, and the final result is the Seers of the Ages, whose works of the past continue to fill us with wonderment as the centuries roll by.

We must notice some of the details that have escaped destruction and descended to us from the distant days. When the ascending Stream of Living Fire passes from one ganglionic center of the spinal cord to the next, its voltage increases, each ganglion acting like electric cells coupled for intensity. Moreover, in each ganglion, or Chakra as they were called by the Ancient Hindus, it liberates and partakes of the quality peculiar to that center, and is then said by the Hindus to "conquer" the Chakra. Hence, in Sanskrit mystical scriptures, far older than the most ancient Hebrew writings, great stress was placed upon the "conquering" of the Seven Chakras, designated as the sacral, the prostatic, the solar, the cardiac, the pharyngeal, the cavernous and the conarium, listed in Chapter 5.

The channels through which the Living Fire flows up to the brain are called nadis, pipes or tubes. They are mentioned in the Bible as Olive Trees, Olive Branches, and Golden Pipes. This fable, known in all countries of the ancient world, appears in Zechariah as follows:

"For who hath despised the day of small things? For they shall rejoice, and shall see the plummet in the hand of Zerubbal with those seven (Chakras we have listed above).

"Then answered I, and said unto him, what are these two olive trees upon the right side of the candlestick of all gold (spinal cord) and upon the left side? And I answered again, and said unto him, What be these two olive branches which through the two golden pipes (Ida and Pingala nadis) empty the golden oil (Living Fire) out of themselves?

"And he answered me and said, knowest thou not what these be? And I said No, my lord. Then said he, these are the two anointed ones (Ida and. Pingala nadis that stand by the Lord (4m) of the Whole earth" (Chapter 4:10-14).

An ancient fable, the interpretation of which is beyond the knowledge of the clergy, who think it deals with their God and his Son Jesus.

As the Living Fire becomes specialized in the Seven Ganglionic Centers, it is termed the Seven Breaths, the Seven Spirits before the Throne, since they become the differentiations of the Great Breath of the Universe. (*Revelation 1:4*).

When the Living Fire begins to rise from the Sacral Plexus at the base of the spine, it flows through the Ida and Pingala nadis, the two Golden Pipes mentioned in the Bible, forming a positive and negative current along the spinal cord.

As these dual currents reach the Cavernous Plexus in the brain, they radiate right and left along the line of the eyebrows. When this occurs, the Neophyte experiences such a mental shock that his mind becomes blank, and he is conscious only of blind terror. This is fableized in the Bible as a great earthquake; the sun became black as sackcloth of hair, and the moon became as blood; the stars fell upon the earth, and the heaven departed as a scroll when it is rolled together, etc. (*Revelation 6:12-11*).

There is also a third current, making the currents triple. The third flows through the Sushumma, a tiny tube passing through the spinal cord, called the Kulamarga (Main Road) or Brahmanadi (Tube of Brahma).

It seems strange that the Luke gospel symbolizes these three currents in the picture which it presents of Jesus on the cross to represent the Sushumna nadi, and on either side of him the two malefactors, who represent the Ida and Pingala nadir (*Luke 23:32*).

There was hardly any limit to what the cunning biblical makers did in the compilation of their Great Book, designed to enthrone the Church and to enslave the masses. No book has ever done humanity so much harm as the Bible.

As the Sushumna current, starting at the sacral plexus, flows along the spinal marrow, its passage through each section thereof corresponding to a sympathetic ganglion, is accompanied by a violent mental shock, or rushing sensation, due to the accession of the force or increased "voltage," until the current reaches the conarium plexus, the Pineal Gland, and thence passes outward through the Brahma-randhra, depicted by the Hindus as a Serpent protruding from the top of man's head.

When this supreme-psycho-bio-physiological process occurs, strange things happen, and they are described in symbol and allegory in chapters 8 to 11 inclusive of Revelation, an interpretation of which appears in *Son Of Perfection* by Professor Hotema.

For instance, due to the increased activation of the glands and cells of the brain, in the initial stage the Seven Psychic Colors of the rainbow are seen. And when the Sushumna current impinges on the brain there follows the lofty Consciousness of the Seer, the mystic Third Eye now becoming, as it has been poetically expressed, "a window into space," and mentioned in the Bible as "a door opened in heaven" (*Revelation 4:1*).

The mystic Third Eye was the Unpaired Eye or the Cyclopean eye of the Ancient Masters, for when thus activated it is an organ of conscious vision, as shown by Professor Hotema in the case of Apollonius and described in *The Mystery Man of the Bible*.

The All-Seeing Eye was sometimes symbolized by the peacock, as this fowl has symbolical eyes in all of its feathers. And in honor of the All-Seeing Eye, the monks of all countries shave off their hair over the spot where it is supposed to look out, that spot of the skull being called the Fonticulus Frontalis, as stated by Professor Hotema in *The Flame Divine*.

In the next stage, as the brain cells are "raised from the dead" (activated) by the Living Fire, the Seven Astral Sounds (of music) are heard in the tense and vibrant aura of the Seer.

In the succeeding stages, seeing and hearing become blended into a single sense, by which colors are heard and sounds are seen, or colors and sounds blend and become united, and are perceived by a sense that is neither seeing nor hearing, but both.

Similarly, the psychic sense of taste and small become unified; and, next, these two senses thus reduced from four, are merged into the interior, intimate sense of touch, which in turn fades into the spistemonic (intellectual) faculty, the great gnostic power of Seership, exalted above all sense-perception, able to cognize eternal realities, a state of Consciousness attained by only a few who are able to rise above the level of the brain-washed, mind-condition masses, and they had better hide and keep silent for the sake of their own safety. Read their writings but seek not to find them in person.

The Bible says that when the Seventh Seal (of the human organism) was opened, there was silence in heaven for about the space of half an hour (*Revelation 8:1*). This silence indicates that at this point the teachings were not for the exoteric, but reserved-strictly for the Neophyte and the esoteric.

We are told that the great importance of the Sushumna Current lies in the fact that those who are taught how to control it can halt the flight of time. For such man, "there shall be time no longer" says the Bible (*Revelation 10:6*).

Vasant G. Role says that by consciously controlling the function of these sympathetic cords, it is possible to put a stop to the katabolic activity of the body, and adds:

"This conscious control over them, which could be achieved only through the Sushumna, suspends the general wear and tear of the tissues of the body, and serves to prolong life. When the Ida and Pingala nadis are thus devitalized by the Sushumna, there is said to exist no night or day for a Yogi" (*Mysterious Kundalini*, page 21).

The Higher Consciousness is the sole theme of Revelation, heavily veiled in symbol and allegory, and that is the reason why this book has never yielded its secret message to the mere man of letters, and why it has ever been a riddle to the brain-washed, mind-conditioned religionist.

The Son Of Light — The student should study Professor Hotema's work, *Son Of Perfection*. He'll be astounded to learn how much the Ancient masters knew about the Endocrines and the higher functions of the body.

In their scriptures, the Hindus postulate Seven, Grades of Being, the four lower, technically denominated the "quaternary," viz., (1) physical body, (2) etheric double, (3) astral vehicle, said to be the seat of the emotions, and (4) lower man's or concrete mentality. These pertain to the phenomenal order, while the three upper ones, the "ternary," viz., (1) higher marnas or abstract intellect, (2) buddhi or intuition, and (3) atma or pure Ego, are noumenal and immortal.

This super-phenomenal triad is symbolized in the Ancient Mysteries by the sun; and the 'journey to the sun" is only a symbolical designation of the process of rendering fully actual, the latent potentialities of these three transcendental microcosmic principles.

Similarly, the "journey to the moon" designates the much less arduous attainment of the highest grade of merely natural evolution, so far at least as human and earthly denizens of our solar system are concerned.

In the Egyptian Mysteries these two goals, "sun" and "moon," correspond respectively to the Kings and Queens Chambers in the Great Pyramid of Cheops, accepting the current identification of that ancient structure as a Temple of Initiation.

When these two symbolical goals are both gained by the Neophyte, according to Blavatsky, it is the result of the concomitant activation of the Pituitary and Pineal Glands.

Manly Hall refers to the ascension of the Living Fire from the Sacral Plexus up to the brain, describing its color as dull-red at first, gradually turning to orange, and then appears as a fine line of yellow fire. He continues:

"These colors extend somewhat outward along the nerves which branch off from the spinal cord between the vertebrae. A little higher the yellow becomes flecked with green, and through the cervical section the stream becomes faintly electric blue.

"Through the Ida and Pingala, the two lateral tubes through the spinal cord, paralleling the central tube (Sushumna on either side called two Olive Trees and Two Witnesses in the Bible — *Zechariah 4:12*, the stream of (living) fire flows up and down incessantly. The farther up it goes, the thinner and less brilliant its hues, but the purer and more beautiful the colors, until finally they meet in a seething, molten mass in the pans of the Medulla Oblongata (of the brain), where the fire begins to permeate the third ventricle (of the brain) and agitate the Pituitary Gland.

"The Pituitary is the negative pole, yet it plays many roles in the development of spiritual (astral) Consciousness. In one sense of the word, it is the initiator, for it raises the candidate (Pineal). Being of feminine polarity, the Pituitary lives up to its dignity of being the eternal temptress.

"In the Egyptian myths, Isis, who symbolizes the Pituitary, conjures Ra, who represents the Pineal, to disclose his sacred name, which he finally does.

...ᴛʜᴇ physiological process by the means of which this is accomplished is worthy of detailed consideration. (Under the influence of the Living Fire) the Pituitary begins to glow faintly and little rippling rings of light flow out from around the gland, gradually fading out a short distance away. As the process continues, the emanating rings around the gland grow stronger. They are not equally distributed around the Pituitary. The circles are elongated on the side facing the third ventricle (of the brain) and extend out in graceful parabolas toward the Pineal. Gradually, as the rings of light become more powerful, they approach every closer to the slumbering eye of Shiva (Pineal), tinting the form of the gland with a golden-orange light and gently coaxing it into activity. Under the benign radiance of the Pituitary Fire, the divine Egg (Pineal) thrills and moves, and the magnificent mystery of occult enfoldment occurs."

Hall has the habit of making his statements somewhat ambiguous, especially for the exoteric. Blavatsky gives plainer details in these words:

"The arc (of light from the Pituitary) mount upward more and more toward the Pineal, until finally the current striking it, just as when the electric current strikes some solid object, the dormant (Pineal) gland is awakened (activated) and set all aglowing with the akasic (electric) fire.

"This is the psycho-physiological illustration of two organs on the physical plane which are the concrete symbols of and represent, respectively, the metaphysical concepts (of the Hindus) called Manes and Buddhi. The latter (Pineal, 7th sense), in order to be conscious (activated on this (physical) plane, needs the more differentiated fire of Manes (Pituitary, 6th sense); but once the sixth sense (Manes, Pituitary) has awakened (activated) the seventh (Buddhi, Pineal), the light which radiates from it (Pineal), illuminates the fields of infinitude; and for that space of time, Man then becomes omniscient. The Past and the Future, Space and Time, disappear (as in dreams) and become for him the Eternal Present."

That is the high level of Seership. In the ancient scrolls, this attainment of the Higher Consciousness was called the Hermetic

Marriage of Sun and Moon, of Hermes and Aphrodite, of L
The biblical makers called it "the marriage of the Lamb" (*Revelsis. 19:2*). The Church calls it the Marriage of Jesus and the Church.

This carefully guarded Sacred Wisdom of the Ancient Masters would have come to us from Egypt, the land of the Winged Globe, had the ancient scrolls not been so completely destroyed by the Church in the 4th, 5th, and 6th centuries. It would not now come to us from India had the Church been able to get there and burn the Hindu scrolls as she did in all the countries she could reach.

Had the ancient Hindu scriptures been lost or destroyed, the world today would perhaps be destitute of the Sacred Wisdom which the Hindus give us dealing with man's Higher Consciousness.

Chapter 14
Macrocosm & Microcosm

"As above, so below," said the Ancient Masters who developed the Ageless Wisdom. They did not teach that a God was above and a man was below.

These Masters discovered that all organizations are constituted of charged particles of one substance which they called Astral Light, consisting of radiation from the Astral Bodies of the Universe. They began with the Atom, the smallest Unit that cannot be broken up by Chemical means. The word Atom is derived from the Greek, meaning "that which cannot be cut up."

Below the Atom are the electrified elements of which the Atom is constituted; and above the Atom are the diverse organizations composed of Atoms.

All formations above the Atom are an aggregation of Atoms, and every quality exhibited by these formations are those of the Atom.

No organized form, including man, can express qualities that are not atomic. Vitality, Consciousness, Mind and Intelligence are atomic qualities, produced by Astral Light acting on and through organized forms, including man.

The great Doctor George W. Crile toiled for nearly thirty years to solve the mystery of Man. The result of his researches appeared in his book in 1926, titled "*A Bipolar Theory of Living Processes.*" In substance, he discovered that –

1. All living creatures are bipolar mechanisms, created, constructed and operated by electrical force (Astral Light).

2. Everything known consists of electricity, exhibited in two phases, (a) Concentrated electricity as particles called electrons and protons, and (b) electricity in rapid motion in the form of radiation.

3. The application of electricity to muscles, glands and nerves of the human body will cause them to perform their natural functions.

4. In structure and function, the unit cell of living forms is adapted to elaborate, conservate, and dissipate electricity. This is also true of the protoplasm itself.

5. Man's body, as a whole, is a bipolar, electric mechanism, bearing the pattern of the unit cells, which cells are constructed on the pattern of the Atom.

6. The normal and abnormal phenomena exhibited by man and animals can be interpreted in electrical terms.

7. When Electrical Conductivity flows from one pole to the other, a living process is present. In the absence of such flow, the living process is absent.

The fundamental qualities exhibited by man are those of the Atom raised to the top level known to us. These qualities are universal in character and unlimited at the source. They are limited at the point of expression by the body through which expressed.

Greater expression depends upon a better organism, or a better condition of the organism.

Man is what his Consciousness is, and he must improve the state of his body to increase the state of his Consciousness.

What is the Mind? Crile said that it is a product, created in the brain by a Power System of Generation and Distribution, consisting of four quadrillion of individual dynamos, and a distribution system vastly greater than all the commercial lines of communication now in existence in the whole world.

Crile further stated that the brain of animals and of man emit short wave and infra-red radiations, which cause the ejection of electrons from the brain protoplasm, and these form the electrical current responsible for our thinking and reasoning processes.

Practically the same findings were presented in 1895, thirty years ahead of Crile, by Sir Wm, Crookes, one of the world's great scientists, who declared that the Atom possesses the Consciousness, Mind and Intelligence to choose its own path, (1) to reject and (2) to select, and possesses the properties of (3) sensation and (4) volition.

This knowledge carries us way back to the Ancient Symbols. These four properties of the Atom had been discovered by the Masters, who symbolized them in their Solar Cross, invented a million years ago. The Masters found that these quaternary qualities of the Atom are responsible for the creation, animation, consciousness and intelligence of everything on the earth.

Not yet have we discovered anything unknown to the Masters. We have only invented a new terminology. They knew the Atom is the Infinite Creator. This is the Creator the Mother Church has taught its dupes to call God.

The Masters said, "As above, so below," meaning the Created, the Microcosm, is truly made in the image and likeness of the Creator, the Macrocosm.

Chapter 15
Time – Eternity

All is one, and one is All. E Pluribus Unum.

The Universe emerged from a huge galaxy of incandescent gas, as explained by Professor Hotema in *Cosmic Creation*, and still is gas in condensed formation. Nothing can be separate from Cosmic Gas as it fills all space.

We have been taught that our physical body is matter, made by a God of the dust of the ground (*Genesis 2:7*). That story was never copied from the ancient scrolls. Matter is composed of chemicals, which are composed of molecules, which are composed of atoms, which are composed of electrons, which are whirling vortices of invisible gaseous substance.

We are prisoners of our Five Senses, and they deceive us. Joshua determined to liberate himself from the prison. So he slew these Five Kings which enslave man, cast them into a cave, and laid great stones in the cave's mouth (*Joshua 10:22-27*).

The Church expounds that allegory as a factual event. The Bible is a book of symbols and allegories. Very little of it should be taken literally.

Due to the deception created by the Five Kings, we live in a world of illusion. We look down a railroad track, and the rails seem to come together in the distance. This is illusion. We know in our Mind that they do not come together. We should not be guided by what we see but by what we know.

Knowledge based on truth dispels illusion. The origin of illusion is ignorance. The facts acquired by the Mind of Creation dispel the ignorance that produces illusion, and illusion vanishes.

For the brain-washed, mind-conditioned masses who are prisoners of their Fire Senses, Eternity is an indefinite concept. It is taken as a limitless extension of Time. But Time has no existence save in the imagination of the ignorant. Time is the subject of Card 14 of the Ancient Tarot. The principal features of the symbolism of this card are designed to appraise the Neophyte that for him the element termed Time is non-existent, says Professor Hotema in his work titled *Land of Light*.

The angel pictured in this card holds in his hands two cups, one of silver and one of gold. Between them there flows a stream that shows all the colors of the rainbow. It cannot be determined by sight from which up the stream flows nor into which is it flowing.

One cup represents the Past, the other, the Future. The stream between them represents the Present. The interpretation of the symbolism shows that Time is not what the prisoner of his Five Senses thinks it is. It is just another illusion.

Everything is; but everything is constantly changing, producing movement from which rises the concept called Time.

Nothing is static but Eternity. There is one eternal Present, the Eternal Now. Time is only a state of perception of the world by our Five Senses.

When the Neophyte attains the Higher Consciousness of Seership the activation of the Seven Ganglionic Centers, he rises above the illusion of Time, and for him the Bible says, 'There shall be Time no longer" (*Revelation 10:6*).

Time is not an entity nor an element per se. Nor is Eternity merely Time indefinitely prolonged. Time is only a mental concept rising from the consciousness of change in the phenomenal world; whereas Eternity is noumenal, changeless, extending neither into the past nor the future, and is therefore, the Immeasurable Present.

In the initial stage of the development of the Higher Consciousness, the seven psychic colors are seen, as we have said. In the next stage the astral sounds are heard. In the succeeding stages, sight and hearing blend into a single sense; and in the final stage, space and time vanish and Past and Future disappear, as in dreams, and become the Eternal Present.

For that man, there is nothing covered that shall not be revealed; and nothing hid that shall not be known (*Matthew 10:26*).

www.ingramcontent.com/pod-product-compliance
Lightning Source LLC
Chambersburg PA
CBHW050541280326
41933CB00011B/1674